University of Iowa Press

Iowa City

University of Iowa Press, Iowa City 52242

Library of Congress Cataloging in Publication Data

Lasansky, Mauricio, 1914–
    Lasansky printmaker.
    "Catalogue of Lasansky prints: 1933–1973, compiled by
John Thein and Phillip Lasansky under the direction of
Mauricio Lasansky."
    Bibliography: p.
    Includes index.
    1. Lasansky, Mauricio, 1914–   I. Thein, John.
II. Lasansky, Phillip. III. Title.
NE594.L3T44   769'.92'4   75–12633
ISBN 0–87745–057–9

To Emilia Barragan and our sons and daughters,
William, Rocio, Leonardo, Jimena, Phillip,
and Thomas, with love—my first forty years
of work as presented in this book.

Contents

A Foreword In the Form of a Letter

Carl Zigrosser

Dear Mauricio,

It is good news that a book written about you, with a catalogue of your works, is now at hand. It is almost forty years—forty-one to be exact—since you first started making prints, and it is fitting that your impressive achievement be placed on permanent record.

I remember when you first arrived in this country on a Guggenheim Fellowship, and I recall the self-portrait which you made the year before you came. You were a very intense young man then, with a great passion for prints. I often wondered about your early Argentine years—you must have been precocious and brilliant. At the age of twenty-two you were already the director of a government art school. You were sophisticated and conversant with modern art movements—but only from books, and not from actual contact with prints or paintings. You experimented with expressionist and surrealist modes. You explored various themes: the pastoral life, the nuances of romantic love, as well as the realities of maternity. Yet in a sense, it was all apprentice work, though executed with great technical virtuosity. You were never trapped into a repetitive formula.

You arrived in New York and discovered the past in graphic art. You spent months and months ecstatically studying the old masters in the print room of the Metropolitan Museum of Art, and gained the distinction of being the only person who systematically went through the whole of that large museum collection. And just as ecstatically you became acquainted with modern art from actual examples of painting, drawing, and printmaking. Didn't you ever have just a twinge of indigestion from all this surfeit of visual impressions? Perhaps not, for you had your creative drive which acted as a sort of governor or balance wheel to regulate your intake. You took what you needed and ignored the rest. Speaking of influences, and I believe we have discussed this once before, it always amuses me why the critics set such great store about analysing the intake and output, the influences which constitute the amalgam of a personal style. To what end, since the bare enumeration of the elements in its structure by no means "explains" the miracle of a flower, for example? Besides, how can we of today, who carry the burden of untold centuries of cultural impressions, ever remain completely uninfluenced?

You decided to remain in the United States and bring your family here. (I know how much your family meant to you, and I can testify how lovable and delightful they are.) You took up teaching again for a livelihood, but you followed your inclination to practise it far away from the big cities and the cliques of the Establishment. In no time, you were a full-fledged professor—in substance but not in deportment—and pupils came flocking to your door. The time you spent teaching—important as it was and is in your life—has little bearing upon your work except in so far as it tended to diminish the quantity of your print *oeuvre*. By all accounts you were and are a mighty good teacher. You never sought to impose your style on your students or make "little Lasanskys" out of them. You were sympathetic and understanding. By introducing them to the past and present in printmaking, you gave them a wide range of choice, and helped them to find their own personal vision. Above all you communicated your enthusiasm, and inculcated a dedication to printmaking almost as great as your own.

You are a mature and successful man now, and you still retain your original intensity of feeling. How have you managed to maintain it in all these years? The pattern of your choice of subject and its treatment is now faintly discernible. In the late 1940s and early 1950s you were partial to the elaborate synthesis of a deeply-felt theme (the moods of *Spring,* the tragic overtones of a *Pieta* or of Lorca's drama *Bodas de Sangre*), all of them highly complex compositions executed in shifting imagery by means of up to nine separate copper plates. The process of development was worked out in large part on the physical plane. You had to drag up images out of the unconscious; you had to build up major motifs and put minor ones in their place; you had to explore fascinating bypaths for relevance, only to suppress them later; you had to test the relation of form to form, of color to color in concrete terms. I asked you why you had to do it the hard way by beating the guts out of the copper over and over again. You replied doggedly that you knew of no other way: you had to think and feel with your hands. I notice, however, that in many of your more recent prints you do not employ such laborious and complicated methods, and that commensurately your themes also have tended to become more unified and direct. For instance, after World War II, your reactions to the revelations of Nazi bestiality found expression in the turmoil and travail of such prints as *Dachau* and the series of *For an Eye an Eye.* Incidentally, I would have assumed that their torment and agony should have provided sufficient catharsis to purge yourself of the obsession. But no, you continued to brood over the subject with savage indignation; in the end you produced *The Nazi Drawings,* that extraordinary group of relatively simple but terrifying and soul-searing drawings, first shown in 1967. Thus, there has been a transition from complexity to simplicity and concentration.

Your so-called self-portraits are among the more enigmatic of your works. When I called attention to your preoccupation with self-portraits, you remarked, "Where did you get that idea? I never told you." In a broad sense of course it is not unusual for an artist—Rembrandt for instance—to make a lot of self-portraits: it is not a question of vanity, it just happens that the model is always at hand when the impulse comes. But you are a special case. The imaginative or psychological portrait is a modern phenomenon in art history. In the past, a typical *corpus* of portraits, such as Van Dyck's *Iconography,* represented merely a collection of likenesses. In recent times, both you and Leonard Baskin have added a new note to the concept. Baskin's portraits are a picture gallery of his own admirations, his act of homage to the artists he loves and respects. With you there is a subtler and more psychological meaning. Your self-portraits, as I see them, might well dramatize various aspects or elements of your own character as they are isolated and exposed. Some aspects may not even be actual components of your personality, but rather a whim or secret impulse which has never come to fruition. In any case, the portraits of yourself and your family provide a fascinating panorama of psychological types executed with power and finesse, with humor and human understanding.

I have lived with one of your prints for years and can vouch for the spell it casts upon the beholder. I do not know whether it is a self-portrait or not, perhaps it is a borderline case. *El Cardinal* is the projection of an extraordinary personage: an old man with intense eyes and sorrowful countenance, a life-sized head and bust of a grizzled man arrayed in the rich red robe of a cardinal. He is more benign than the Cardinal of the Establishment in *The Nazi Drawings,* but a cardinal nonetheless, a Cardinal of the Inquisition, a forthright and searching perfectionist with a touch of Don Quixote and St. John of the Cross. I once jokingly related to you the effect he had on me: he became the embodiment of my literary conscience. When I neglect my work and do not fulfill my quota of writing for the day or week, I find myself slinking past his picture trying to escape the gaze of his sorrowful accusing eyes! That of course was a *jeu d'esprit,* but there is no doubt about the powerful emotional impact conveyed by this print upon me and others who have seen it. But why should I go on talking about prints? Let the prints speak of themselves!

I look forward to the completion of this book. But most of all I look forward to your retirement from active teaching. I want to see what the old maverick and master printmaker, Mauricio, will do next!

Good luck and all good wishes.

Carl

The Prints of Mauricio Lasansky

by Alan Fern

Mauricio Lasansky has been making prints for more than forty years. First in his native Argentina, then in New York City, and (for almost thirty years) in Iowa City, he has devoted himself to exploring the expressive possibilities of the graphic arts. In so doing, he has left behind a series of prints that are among the most powerful and impressive works by a contemporary artist in any medium, and he has done as much as any individual to establish printmaking as a meaningful concern for the serious student of the arts. As a result, among the important printmakers of the younger generation, and the teachers of printmaking in scores of American art schools and universities, are scores of Lasansky students.

This is not the first publication devoted to the prints of Lasansky, and, since he is working with unremitting vigor, it will not be the last. The present book presents the existing *corpus* of Lasansky's prints, in as much detail and with as much accuracy as the compilers could muster; since Lasansky himself was fully involved with the process of cataloguing, the entries that follow are of the greatest possible authenticity, based on his memory and records, and corrected through consultation of as many published sources as could be examined.

Lasansky has been generous in sharing his ideas with the author of this essay, and what follows is an attempt to give the reader a reasonably accurate account of Lasansky's thoughts about his work and about art in general. Among a considerable number of useful publications on Lasansky, perhaps the most extensive and certainly the most useful is the essay and catalogue published in 1960 by Carl Zigrosser. If some of the statements in these pages reflect Zigrosser's text, it is

because his work was so intelligent and thorough that no writer about Lasansky could better express the points Zigrosser makes. Since that catalogue was published, however, Lasansky's work has taken a new direction: the prints have become more complex in color; a greater number of plates are used in each print; and there has been a remarkable change in mood and imagery.

Lasansky himself has characterized the development in his work as an evolution from romantic, to classic, to "contemporary" to—or back to—humanism; schematic as it is, his account of his stylistic growth is revealing for what it says about his attitude towards his work. The subject has remained the human being— his condition, his relationships, his society—but the great change has been in Lasansky's command of the visual arts, and in his relationship to the work of other artists. In his full maturity, Lasansky expresses his art in terms of its themes; until then, he had thought of it in relationship to stylistic conceptions.

Mauricio Lasansky was born in Buenos Aires, Argentina, in 1914, the son of an immigrant printer of banknote engravings. Mauricio's father was born in Eastern Europe (his country of origin has been described, at various times, as Russia, Poland, and Lithuania), and had worked at his trade in Philadelphia before settling in Argentina. Buenos Aires, during Mauricio's formative years, was a reasonably lively cultural center, supporting a number of theatres, many serious musicians, and an academy of art; it was oriented to Europe, but generally conservative in taste.

Lasansky's first interest was in music, which he studied seriously until his fourteenth year, when a slight (and—as it turned out—temporary) hearing impairment caused him to change to the study of sculpture. He graduated in 1933, at the age of nineteen, and commenced postgraduate work in printmaking at the Superior School of Fine Arts.

Since he had been familiar with the processes of printing from hearing his father and an uncle talk about their work as engravers, Lasansky found printmaking particularly sympathetic. Almost at once, he worked with an assured hand. His earliest prints were in relief etching (according to Zigrosser, his father had known the technique in Europe), and in linoleum cuts, but before long Lasansky was working in drypoint. His drypoints were unconventional both in technique and in conception. Lasansky used the drypoint needle to create fully modeled tones, in contrast to the linear quality traditionally associated with the technique, and worked to far larger scale than is common in drypoint. Moreover, while the first relief prints he made were direct social statements, stressing the grim poverty of ordinary life, the drypoints—a few years later—are lyrical and imaginative, relying on surrealist juxtapositions of interior and exterior space, objects in different scale, and interpenetrations of one form by another.

These early works are consciously poetic; many of Lasansky's friends and intellectual heroes were poets and writers, who used language in the Spanish tradition with a rich employment of metaphors, strange juxtapositions of objects and ideas, and the frequent expression of states of mind in similes—equivalents for feelings being made vivid by reference to objects. Despite the richness of this aspect of his cultural life,

Lasansky felt that in the visual arts Argentina was isolated. Exhibitions of work from abroad were infrequent in Buenos Aires, and scarcer still in Cordoba (where he moved in 1936, to direct the Free School of Fine Arts), and such work as was shown reflected the more conservative official French and British taste, lacking the more daring and experimental work discussed and reproduced in the few serious art publications that came into the country from abroad. Though his work was exhibited and recognized, and though he had been able to get a responsible teaching position while still in his early twenties, Lasansky dreamed of finding a way to become familiar with the larger world of the arts.

His dream took a step towards realization when Francis Henry Taylor, on a South American trip in 1940, saw his work, met Lasansky, and recommended him for a Guggenheim Fellowship to study printmaking. As director of the Metropolitan Museum of Art, Taylor was an influential and respected sponsor, so in 1943 Lasansky arrived in New York and commenced two projects: a systematic study of the entire(!) print collection of the Metropolitan Museum, and technical study with Stanley William Hayter in the New York "Atélier 17."

A few years earlier, Hayter had established a remarkable workshop in Paris, called "Atélier 17" after its address on the Rue Campagne Première (and retaining its name thereafter, no matter where it was located), devoted to the discovery of the technical and aesthetic possibilities of the intaglio printmaking processes. The studio was a center for serious experimentation in intaglio printmaking, and many of Hayter's artist friends came to apply his techniques to their own work; Picasso, Miró, Chagall, and many others of international renown, engraved and printed at Atélier 17 in Paris, and those who found themselves in New York after the outbreak of World War II came to work with their old friend.

Thus it was that Lasansky, newly arrived from Argentina, found himself working next to artists of the international avant-garde in New York, as well as joining a number of younger artists in becoming exposed to Hayter's particular approach to print-making. Coupled with his exhaustive study of the print collections at the Metropolitan Museum, his approach to art changed totally. Lasansky came to realize at this time that the physical resistance of the copper plate and the precision, tautness, and varying depths of the directly cut line in the copper were the most singular characteristics of printmaking, and he responded instinctively to the tension and control he was able to exert as the forms emerged in the process of engraving. In New York he explored new ways of imposing textured areas on the plate, and of creatively using retroussage to bring brilliant white accents into a composition. Perhaps, too, the beauty of the engraved plate attracted the now-latent sculptor in Lasansky; to this day he takes visible physical pleasure in the varied surfaces and channels of the plates, which he views as objects in their own right apart from their use as printing masters.

The presence of such contemporary masters as Miró and Chagall, during Lasansky's time in New York, must have contributed notably to his development, as did his exposure to the prints of Picasso, with whom Hayter had worked closely in Paris. These artists had a profound effect on Lasansky's imagery, and in various prints of the later 1940s and 1950s, he clearly displays his debt to Hayter's abstract web of curving and spiky lines, Chagall's airborne figures, and Picasso's agonized Guernica victims. While in Argentina, Lasansky's poetic analogies had been expressed in reasonably conventional drawing, even when certain surrealistic elements came into his compositions, now he adopted a freer approach to the human figure and a stronger sense of line, and liberated himself from the profusion of observed detail that had been so much a part of his earlier drypoints. The tonality that was to characterize his work for the next fifteen years appeared at this time, too.

In this last respect, he owed a debt to Goya, and to the other Spanish artists for whom he felt such a deep affinity at this point in his career. If the days in Atélier 17 had brought him into touch with living work by live artists, his studies at the Metropolitan Museum put the powerful work of the past directly into his hands, often in examples of unsurpassed quality. Whereas, the prints of Goya in reproduction might be most compelling for their imagery, the physical richness of color was inescapable in actual examples of his aquatints and etchings, and impressed Lasansky profoundly.

Realizing that the possibilities for further development of his own career were far better in the United States than in Argentina, and feeling more than ever that the atmosphere of Cordoba was stiflingly provincial, Lasansky made up his mind to try to remain in North America. In 1944 he requested, and received, an extension of his Guggenheim Fellowship, sent for his wife and children, and discussed with Henry Allen Moe, the president of the Guggenheim Foundation, the prospect of making a new career. There appeared to be two possibilities: to stay in New York, and compete with scores of artists for attention and patronage, or to live and work in a smaller center where his attention would be less diverted by concerns marginal to his work as artist. Having preferred to live in a smaller city in Argentina, Lasansky felt that he would prefer to make the same choice here; moreover, printmaking was anything but an established career for an artist in the United States, in 1945.

It may seem hard to believe, in this day of flourishing print workshops, impressive print exhibitions, and the virtually universal teaching of printmaking in universities and art schools, that before the Second World War printmaking was widely regarded as the province of a few, specialized artists, appealing to a few, finicky collectors. Not many museums had serious print rooms, and even if prints were among their collections they mounted few exhibitions of the graphic arts. The Federal Arts Projects established printmaking workshops in several cities during the depression of the 1930s, and many artists were exposed to printmaking techniques thereby, but somehow even these projects failed to engender a truly widespread and innovative interest in printmaking.

This is not to say that American artists never made prints. Many made them abroad, as Whistler, Mary Cassatt, and others had done in the nineteenth century, and as Feininger and Max Weber did in the twentieth. Others, like "the Eight" in New York, Thomas Hart Benton in Missouri, and Grant Wood in Iowa, fre-

quently turned to the print to record their responses to the American scene. Benton and Wood, however, preferred to work in lithography, with the aid of experienced printers, so they remained more concerned with their subjects than with the technical aspects of their prints. While this kept them from creating anything in printmaking that was different from their painting, it did at least remind other artists and collectors that the print was a valid medium of expression, not just a reproductive tool, or pastime for the conservative purist.

In the later 1940s, when education in the arts was beginning to expand after the war, several far-sighted administrators recognized the potential importance of printmaking in the art curriculum, and Lester D. Longman, at the University of Iowa in Iowa City, was one of those prescient individuals. At Iowa the creative arts were given a unique place among the academic disciplines, and were regarded as entirely proper concerns for graduate study. University president Virgil Hancher appears to have fully realized that this was an area in which the university could take an innovative stand, and the development of the writers workshop, music school, and art department under his term attracted widespread attention.

The first artist-in-residence at Iowa who reflected this embryonic interest in printmaking was the German-born Emil Ganso, a vital and gregarious man, self-taught as a printmaker, but committed to the graphic arts as a basic medium of expression in the visual arts, not just as an adjunct to painting. Unfortunately, in April 1941 Ganso died suddenly. As soon as the war ended, Professor Longman set about to find a successor.

Just at this time, Henry Allen Moe was trying to help Lasansky find a teaching position away from New York, and he persuaded Hancher to consider Lasansky as a successor to Ganso. Professor Longman had other candidates in mind, but agreed to meet the young, obscure immigrant in New York for an interview. Lasansky recalls that their meeting took place at a Whitney Museum opening, where they somehow found a quiet corner in which to talk. The next year, Lasansky went to Iowa "for one year." He has been there ever since.

Lasansky is not a large man, and he prefers to speak in a quiet voice. What he accomplished in his first years at Iowa, therefore, speaks volumes for his determination, his powerful will, and the intellectual equipment he brought to the task, for he could not have physically awed or vocally harangued his colleagues enough to bring them to share his understanding of what prints could be, and printmaking do, for the young artists being trained at the university. He established an extensive studio, found presses and equipment, set up working procedures, and by experiment discovered the right blend of personal direction and forced independence to teach the student appropriate habits and attitudes without making him a slavish imitator of his teacher. Lasansky's own studio was traditionally closed to the student, to give the artist the time and place to develop his own work without fear that it would exert undue influence on the student, yet he spent hours each day helping the students to solve their own problems and to master the difficult craft of intaglio.

He turned out to be a teacher of genius, and the students in those postwar years (frequently returning veterans of uncommonly serious purpose, to make up for the "lost" war years) helped to create an atmosphere of serious endeavor, strong personalities, and lively exploration.

Since even before his time in New York, Lasansky had settled upon the metal plate as the ideal medium for printmaking, and now he made intaglio printing the central focus of his curriculum. It is not that he has anything against the woodcut or the lithograph, but rather that the discipline imposed by the metal seems to have at once a liberating and a controlling effect on the artist. Once one has learned to command the material, in Lasansky's view, then one is freely able to create in full consciousness of where the process will lead; other techniques may be too easy, too similar to other manipulations in the visual arts, to yield the strong character he likes to see in prints.

In his first years at Iowa, Lasansky undertook work in two directions. First, there was a continuing series of self-portraits and portraits of his family, often playful, sometimes theatrical, but always exuding gentle sympathy and warmth. In contrast, there were brooding, more abstract prints, like the series *For an Eye an Eye,* or *Bodas de Sangre,* with complex iconography, intentional echoes of Picasso (of the Guernica period) and Chagall, and a sense of violence imposed upon humanity. Whether confronting the plight of Spain, the heartbreak of war, or the dignity of children, Lasansky maintains a sobriety in these works through his use of the frontal or direct profile representation of the human figure, and through his subtle use of colors in combination with deep, dark tonalities.

Both the formal and the iconographic development of Lasansky's work reached a climax in *The Nazi Drawings* of 1961–66. For Lasansky, this was both an artistic watershed and an emotional catharsis, during which he turned his major creative energies away from the print to give physical embodiment to his seething reaction against the Nazi holocaust. He saw the unleashing of bestiality in Germany during the 1930s and 1940s as a brutal attack on man's dignity, and felt it carried the potential seeds of man's self-destruction. Elements of his earlier prints reappear in *The Nazi Drawings,* but transformed into powerful visual equivalents for the perpetrators and victims of the tragedy as well as the paralyzed bystanders.

When Lasansky emerged from the crucible of *The Nazi Drawings,* his prints again dealt with the child, the woman, the bishop (or the cardinal, often in a less morbid context or a more optimistic vein), but the fragmentation of form, new treatment of color, and lighter tonal environment of the drawings now transformed his prints.

He has described one of the basic characteristics of each artist as residing in the use of scale, especially in the relationship of the size of the figure to the picture area. Here Lasansky has kept to a remarkably consistent course, as if to prove his own point; the figure is always large on the plate, and the plate is often so large that the figure is represented at almost life size. Moreover, the figure is kept at a dignified distance from the viewer, as people in conversation conventionally assume a certain distance from one another. Through these means, Lasansky's prints set up a very specific kind of conversation with the viewer; the figures he creates exist in a world of his particular invention.

Although color has often been present in Lasansky's work, the sense of the prints of the 1940s and 1950s is almost monochromatic—with richness provided through the introduction of few hues in each print. With the prints of the past decade, however, Lasansky has brightened and complicated his colors, taking pleasure in the luminosity and transparency of the ink over the brilliant white of his paper. He has likened his recent use of color to working in fresco, and he takes care not to lose the freshness of a color by deadening it against an unsympathetic tone.

Along with the growing complexity of color, the recent prints are composed of a considerable number of plates of varying sizes, composed elaborately on the bed of his enormous press after a complex series of inkings. These prints are large, and the mechanical difficulty of realizing them is considerable, so the appearance of freshness and spontaneity they preserve is testimony to Lasansky's technical command of his medium. The more recent prints seem to show Lasansky turning from a Spanish to an Italianate mood, from blacks and browns to the primaries, from mysterious shadows to open emotion. This may seem particularly curious in his very latest work, dealing with Mexican themes (inspired, no doubt, by the pleasure taken by the artist and his family in the second residence they maintain in Mexico), but it may be a fair comment that the Mexican light, spirit, and civilization are as different from the Italian as is the Spanish. In any case, the gods and natural presences of the recent prints have little in common with the early Argentinian work of Lasansky, beyond their shared sense of scale and human representation. The work of the last two years displays a freedom as well as a fluency that indicate Lasansky has liberated himself from his earlier influences without abandoning the discoveries those influences had led him to make.

In a sense, Lasansky's whole life has been a search for freedom. He has sought political, academic, and intellectual freedom, and he has labored to free himself from the physical restraints of his medium. His work expresses these two aspects of freedom: the masterly fluency of a printmaker, and the insistence that dignity and humanity triumph over meanness and bestiality.

To describe someone as a "master," in the sense that he has subdued his materials and ceased to struggle with the problems that interfere with expression through his craft, also may suggest another sense of the word— that implied in the phrase "master and apprentice." This is an unfashionable role for a pedagogue today, and it is a relationship that Lasansky has consciously tried to avoid—not always with success. His personality and temperament are so compelling that many of his students either have been overwhelmed or have reacted to him for a time, but when this passes, as it has with his successful students, it can be seen that Lasansky's emphatic pedagogy has had its desired effect. What he has tried to do, above all, at Iowa, is to surround himself with a group of serious fellow artists, less experienced and less sure of themselves than he is, and to give them a sense of value, a series of basic insights into the relationships between vision and materials, and the example that a confident artist can be a generous teacher without losing his identity. His

former students are not only printmakers of note, but teachers of distinction.

Apart from Lasansky's immense contribution as a teacher, he has become one of this country's most powerful creators of images. He never turned away from the representation of the human figure, even when abstract expressionism was the order of the day, but retained a humanist's orientation making man the measure of all other things. Although not a political artist in the usual sense of the word, he has always displayed a sense of outrage, culminating in *The Nazi Drawings,* at the all too frequent displays of imbecility and inhumanity with which he has been confronted. He has leavened his powerful imagery and strong outrage with works of tenderness and intimacy, and with a remarkable series of psychological studies of himself displaying various states of mind ranging from amusement to misery.

His is a rich art, drawing from literature, politics, theatre, the dance, reflecting an affinity for the Latin civilizations, and a delight in the masks and costumes in which people have cloaked their roles in life. Most of all, though, Mauricio Lasansky has been instrumental in establishing the print in America as a viable, independent art form, and creating prints of unmistakable individual character that are, above all, eloquent visual statements. He has been industrious, but, since his prints evolve gradually through many stages, not prolific. He has been imaginative and individual, but not obscure or idiosyncratic. Most of all, he has mastered his medium thoroughly, and he has transmitted a sense of the value of that mastery to all who have seen his prints or studied with him.

Twenty-four Color Reproductions

46. *El Presagio*

76. *Spring*

81. My Wife

83. Pieta

94. *España*

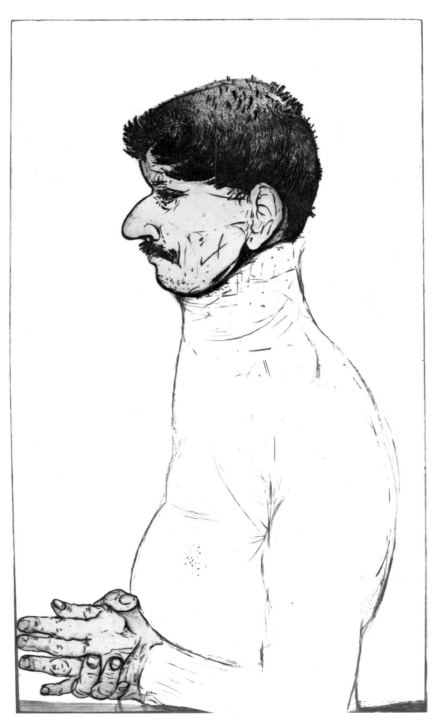

95. *Self-Portrait*

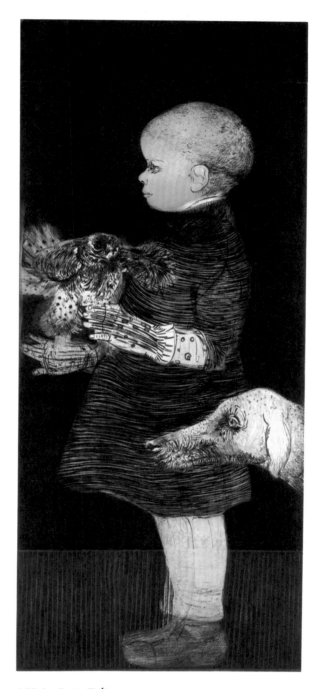

109A. *Luis Felipe*

110B. Boy with Cat

113. *Portrait of a Young Artist*

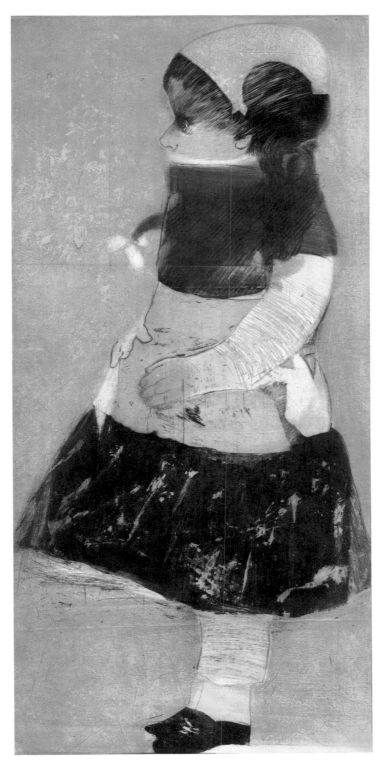

115. *Amana Girl*

117. *Woman with Lute*

119. *Pope and Cardinal*

121. *Amana Girl in Red Winter Coat*

122. *Amana Girl in Black Winter Coat*

125. *Lady in Blue*

129. *Little Girl*

38

133. *Oriental Image*

134A. *Bleeding Heart*

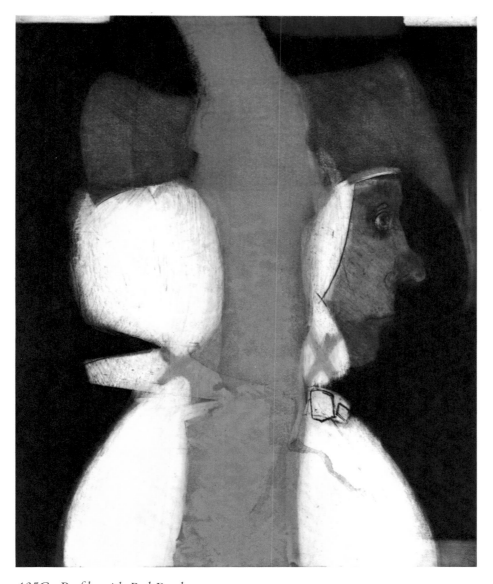

135C. *Profile with Red Band*

34A. Bleeding Heart (detail)

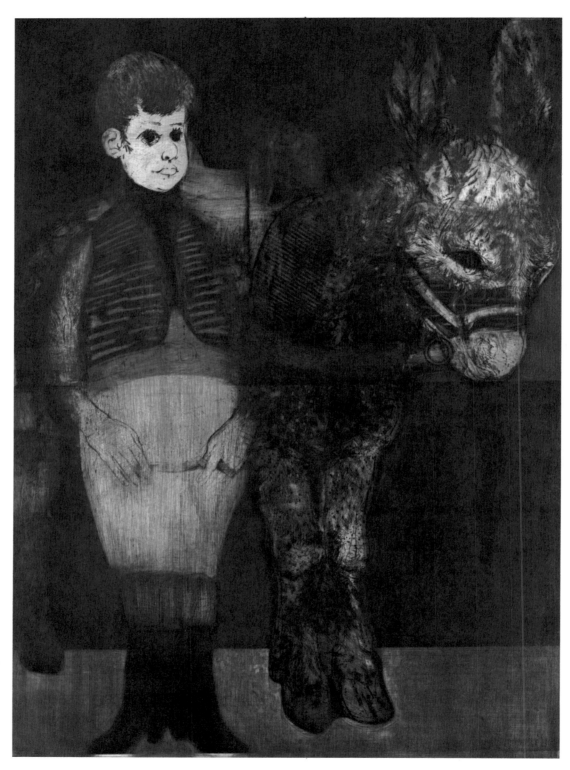

136. Boy with Burro

139. Quetzalcoatl

140A. *Young Nahua Dancer*

Lasansky: Printmaker

The Catalogue

Compiled by John Thein and Phillip Lasansky
under the direction of Mauricio Lasansky,
with an introduction by Stephen Rhodes.

The order of the catalogue is chronological,
with the exception of the early years
when precise information is not available. When
a print has not been examined, "No impression
available" is recorded.

Themes and Images in Mauricio Lasansky's Prints

by Stephen Rhodes

This illustrated catalogue of Mauricio Lasansky's prints allows us to examine his imagery in its broadest context. Like a retrospective exhibition, the catalogue allows us both the hindsight of history and the continuing presence of the work. We can watch the development of themes and motifs, and sense the growth of the mature artistic personality. Such examination reveals the integrity of Lasansky's creative personality throughout his long career.

Only rarely does Lasansky's work reflect the formal developments of modern French art, which have had such great influence upon postwar artists in the United States. His prints have remained faithful to the representational tradition, confronting us with images of dignified and sophisticated individuals on the one hand, and the human horrors wrought by twentieth-century society and religion on the other. In addition, Lasansky has adopted a subjective viewpoint in order to preserve a conception of dignity and humanistic values in his work. This orientation should not be confused with aesthetic nostalgia in contrast to what has been called the tough, uncompromising attitude of the New York School. It is a rigorous use of motifs from traditional sources, creating a visual record of an alternately dignified and brutalized humanity unique to the mid-twentieth century.

The nature of this subjective orientation becomes clear in an examination of Lasansky's New York period. *La Lagrima* is the artist's visual response to his own emotional environment. The print is noteworthy for its experimental use of the soft-ground technique and the early use of color in Lasansky's printmaking career. It is based upon a drawing executed by the artist's young son, recreated in the upper right-hand corner of the print. It shows the effect of the family's separation, the father working in New York while his wife and children remain behind in Argentina. Through the use of this intensely personal imagery, Lasansky translates the most subjective emotional experiences into visual form.

The series *For an Eye an Eye* is a dramatic development of this personal orientation toward subject matter. The images are theatrical rather than abstract, with characters acting out a brutal drama in four variations. The prints all began with the same initial drawing, each evolving to a different emotional pitch. The violence and brutality suggested in the abstract print *Dachau* has become more specific, and the figures have adopted symbolic overtones due to their theatrical presentation. There are also references to the artist's earlier work. A violinist appears in Plate IV, perhaps a demonic transformation of the elegant *El Presagio* executed in Argentina.

The theme of dehumanization seen in *For an Eye an Eye* is slowly transformed over a period of ten years. The subject becomes progressively internalized, and the symbolic elements come into play in greater complexity. The immediacy of *For an Eye an Eye* is slowly rejected as a constant imagery develops toward a more monumental statement. The recurring element is the dramatic, theatrical presentation of figures whose identity and interrelationships remain enigmatic. This development is nearly a linear progression, as several prints examined in chronological order will show clearly: *Pieta* (1948), *Near East* (1948), *Bodas de Sangre* (1951), *Firebird* (1952–53), *Sagittarius* (1955).

The climax to this development is reached suddenly in *España*. The tragic mood slowly developed in the preceding years achieves a new monumentality through a simplification of formal elements. *España*, together with its companion *The Vision*, unifies all the elements seen developing through the late forties and early fifties. Iconographically, it includes the figure of the horse and rider, which first appears in *El Cid*, and later in *Firebird* and *Sagittarius*. The woman and child seem to derive from *Bodas de Sangre* and *Firebird*, and the woman's attitude of grief in *España* also recalls *La Lagrima*. The haunting rider has lost his enigmatic aspect, becoming an apocalyptic figure of death. This recalls the earlier *Pieta*. Finally, the title *España* links the print symbolically and formally to Spain and Spanish painting, fully developing a relationship suggested in *El Cid* twelve years earlier. *España* marks Lasansky's first utilization of Velazquez' concept of pictorial monumentality, and it firmly links this whole thematic development to Spanish art.

From this point, Lasansky begins to incorporate thematic, iconographic, and stylistic elements of Spanish painting into his images. He will develop the tonal and coloristic elements of his prints with increasing complexity until his images bear no visual relationship to the traditional concept of a print. This development can be seen technically as the translation of the formal features of Spanish painting into the intaglio medium, especially in the color harmonies, the scale and attitude of the figure, the figure-ground relationship, and the use of value transparency as the basic pictorial device.

Lasansky's portrayal of his family in an idealized and sophisticated attitude suggests a comparison with Velazquez' portrayal of members of the Spanish royal family. But as spectators, our interpretation of Lasansky's figures is more difficult. Their identification as members of the artist's family again calls attention to the basically subjective orientation of Lasansky's art. These portraits often appear as the humanistic ideal, the embodiment of personal dignity, when set against the dehumanized figures of his other work. In this respect, Lasansky's *oeuvre* is like a morality play, with the cast clearly identified at their respective ends of the scale of moral values.

The theme of dehumanizing violence culminating in *España* in 1956 does not reappear until *The Nazi Drawings* a decade later. And when it does reappear, it is with a new immediacy and subjective viewpoint, which recalls the *For an Eye an Eye* cycle. *Pope with Crying Boy* and *Bleeding Heart* are two prints which take up this theme again. An examination of states of *Bleeding Heart* will show how this theme developed. The early state shows an internalized, subjective concept in a low-key, moody tonality. This is transformed to an image in the final state which literally explodes. It completely reverses Lasansky's earlier development of the *España* concept. The final state of *Bleeding Heart* shows a new concern for immediacy, now communicated through formal rather than iconographic means. The result is a graphic violence which threatens the spectator rather than the subject of the print.

This direct confrontation of the spectator developed during the sixties in a series of prints which are concerned with a definite religious iconography. This series begins with individual portraits, similar in format to the family portraits, but presenting both degenerate and idealized figure types. These individual religious portraits were then combined into full-length figure compositions which feature a new, expansive spatial concept in large scale with large areas of white. The figures in *Pope with Crying Boy* are presented in a graphic rather than a pictorial space which expands and engages the spectator directly instead of drawing him inward. This new space and expansive feeling then develops dramatically in *Oriental Image, Bleeding Heart,* and *Quetzalcoatl.*

These later images also mark a new direction in Lasansky's printmaking technique. Up to this point, his prints can be seen as development of a full-scale image and painterly color, utilizing a synthesis of all traditional intaglio techniques: soft-ground etching, aquatint, drypoint, engraving, line etching. These techniques were combined in a technical approach which allowed Lasansky to freely alter the composition of the print while the work was in progress. The artist could explore the full compositional and iconographic possibilities of a subject over a period of time, an approach similar to the techniques of traditional oil painting, where overpainting and alteration made possible a full richness in tonality and the development of complex formal relationships suggested by the work in progress. Lasansky was able to develop this kind of free execution in his intaglio technique through the use of the scraper as a major printmaking tool—a new approach to the medium. Rembrandt and Rouault often show a similar interest in the long-term development and alteration of the image on copper, but Lasansky has made it a central part of his technique.

The latest prints extend this technical approach, as they begin to explore a fragmented image achieved by the fragmentation of the actual printing surface, the copper plate. This new approach reaches its greatest complexity in *Quetzalcoatl,* which consists of fifty-four separate plates, many cut into irregular shapes. Technical elements in this print appear as early as *Pope and Cardinal,* which utilizes an inkless embossment and the separation of the master plate into several jigsaw-like pieces which follow the outlines of the figures. *Pope with Crying Boy* marks the first appearance of large white areas and the use of a small plate as a symbol (the cross on the Pope's robe). The technical development is then dramatic in *Oriental Image* and *Bleeding Heart,* which fully fragments all elements of the composition. It is a free manipulation of the initial image to achieve a more synthesized result. The full extension of this idea to the material, fragmenting the copper plate itself, is a radical variation of a traditional approach.

These new formal elements are accompanied by a new interest in specifically religious themes. Lasansky's earlier concern for dignity and a humanistic ideal has been replaced by exploration of an intense personal spiritualism. The religious prints remain linked to Spanish themes and Spanish visual formats. But while most present degenerate figure types, some portray unique figures of intense spiritual experience. The *Gregorian Chanter,* for example, is not a corrupt figure but a strongly spiritual one. His intensity recalls two portraits executed much earlier: *Self Portrait* (1950) and *My Son Leonardo.* The link with the family portraits is also seen in *Amish Boy,* a religious innocent whose features resemble *My Boy* and the figures in *Cena* from the Argentina period.

Bleeding Heart is noteworthy as a development of the explicit religious themes in *Pope and Cardinal*. The imagery is basically the traditional representation of Father, Son, and Holy Ghost. But Lasansky's Trinity appears ominous in its dehumanized and threatening form. The black marks suggest that the image has been torn or used as a target, and the figures display a frantic emotional intensity. The central figure, with his skull helmet from *The Nazi Drawings,* confronts us with a fanatical gaze, totally without rationality. His hands thrust the bleeding heart out at the spectator in a final, desperate gesture.

A strong didactic element characterizes *Bleeding Heart.* This same didactic quality can be seen, in varying degrees, throughout Lasansky's career. His dedication as a teacher has often been noted as an aside to his achievements as an artist. But the didactic orientation in his art unites two aspects of his career. The element of confrontation between image and spectator becomes stronger in the later work, and the didactic nature of the statement becomes more apparent. There is the implicit assertion that this is art's ultimate concern. Lasansky is demonstrating, through his work, his posture as an artist in today's society—a person concerned with the quality of life about him, and the state of his own soul.

Catalogue of Lasansky Prints: 1933–1973

Catalogue Key

Title:

Date:

Edition:

Size:
  Dimensions are given
  in inches (in.)
  and centimeters (cm.),
  with height
  listed first.

Technique:

Number of plates:

Notes:

Zigrosser Catalogue No.
  taken from
  *American Federation
  of Arts Catalogue
  on Mauricio Lasansky*

1. Velorio
1933
Ed. 10

	in.	cm.
H.	12- 6/16	31.4
W.	11-12/16	29.8

Zincografia
Zinc plate printed in relief with black ink on newspaper. The type on the newspaper makes a texture and also a gray.
Plate destroyed.
Zig. No. 8

2. Maternidad
1933
Ed. 10

	in.	cm.
H.	11-4/16	28.7
W.	11-9/16	29.4

Zincografia
Zinc plate printed in relief with black ink on newspaper. Type on the newspaper makes a texture and also a gray.
Plate destroyed.
Zig. No. 9

3. Meeting

1933
Ed. 10
Size unknown
Zincografia
Relief etching on zinc.
Note: No impression available.
Plate destroyed.
Zig. No. 11

4. Drama

1933(?)
Ed. unknown
Size unknown
Etching.
Zinc plate.
Note: No impression available.
Plate destroyed.
Zig. No. 3

54

5. Campesinos

1934
Ed. 10

	in.	cm.
H.	16-12/16	42.6
W.	15- 8/16	39.4

Drypoint.

One plate printed twice; first run in sienna, second run in Prussian blue.

Zinc plate.

Plate destroyed.

Zig. No. 1

(From the private collection of Harold Rayburn)

6. Herido

1934
Ed. unknown
Size unknown
Etching.
Zinc plate.
Note: No impression available.
Plate destroyed.
Zig. No. 2

7. *Dolor*

1934(?)
Ed. unknown
Size unknown
Etching.
Zinc plate.
Note: No impression available.
Plate destroyed.
Zig. No. 4

8. *Prisioneros*

1934
Ed. 10

	in.	cm.
H.	11-14/16	30.2
W.	9-12/16	24.9

Zincografía
Relief etching on zinc.
Printed in black.
Plate destroyed.
Zig. No. 13

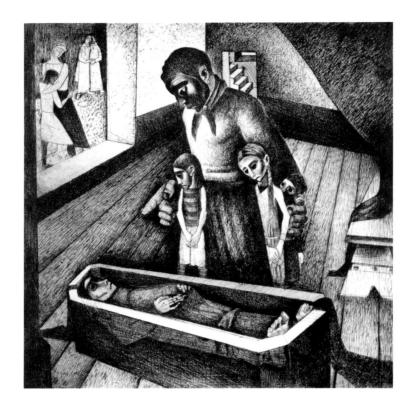

9. *Huerfaños*

1934(?)

Ed. unknown

in.	cm.
H. 15-14/16	40.4
W. 15- 4/16	38.7

Drypoint.

Printed in black.

Zinc plate.

Plate destroyed.

Zig. No. 19

10. *Cosecha*

1935

Ed. 5(?)

Size unknown

Etching.

Zinc plate.

Note: No impression available.

Plate destroyed.

Zig. No. 6

11. *Simbolo*
1935
Ed. 10
Size unknown
Zincografia
Relief etching on zinc.
Note: No impression available.
Plate destroyed.
Zig. No. 10

12. *Suicidas*
1935
Ed. 10(?)

	in.	cm.
H.	11- 2/16	28.3
W.	13-10/16	34.6

Deep bite etching. Printed in umber.
Zinc plate.
Plate destroyed.
Zig. No. 39

58

13. Cena

1935

Ed. 10

	in.	cm.
H.	17-14/16	44.3
W.	20- 9/16	52.2

Linoleum cut.
Printed in black on manila paper.
Block destroyed.
Zig. No. 29

14. Fin

Date unknown

Ed. unknown

Size unknown

Zincografia
Relief etching on zinc.
Note: No impression available.
Plate destroyed.
Zig. No. 12

15. *Compesino Hablando*

Date unknown
Ed. unknown
Size unknown
Zincografia
Relief etching on zinc.
Note: No impression available.
Plate destroyed.
Zig. No. 14

16. *Tragedia*

Date unknown
Ed. unknown
Size unknown
Lithograph.
Note: No impression available.
Zig. No. 15

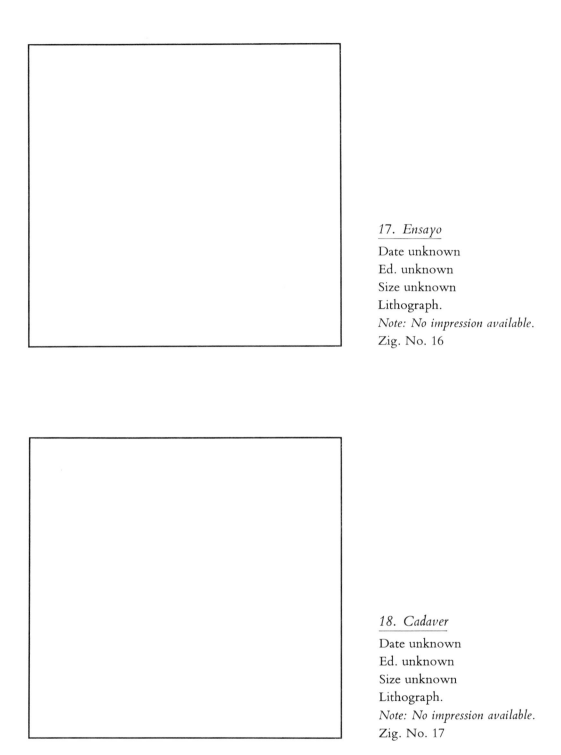

17. *Ensayo*
Date unknown
Ed. unknown
Size unknown
Lithograph.
Note: No impression available.
Zig. No. 16

18. *Cadaver*
Date unknown
Ed. unknown
Size unknown
Lithograph.
Note: No impression available.
Zig. No. 17

19. Cabeza

Date unknown
Ed. unknown
Size unknown
Lithograph.
Note: No impression available.
Zig. No. 18

20. Peladora de Caña

1936
Ed. 8

	in.	cm.
H.	22- 6/16	56.9
W.	17-11/16	45.0

Etching.
Printed in black on warm, gray paper.
Zinc plate.
Plate destroyed.
Zig. No. 7

21. Changos
1936(?)
Ed. 10

	in.	*cm.*
H.	16	40.6
W.	19-2/16	49.9

Linoleum cut.
Printed in black.
Note: Two prints on oriental paper.
This type of paper has a tendency to
wrinkle; measurements of the two
prints on oriental paper will vary.
Block destroyed.
Not listed in Zigrosser catalogue.

22. Tierra
Date unknown
Ed. unknown
Size unknown
Drypoint.
Note: No impression available.
Plate destroyed.
Zig. No. 20

23. Campesinos

Date unknown
Ed. unknown
Size unknown
Drypoint.
Zinc plate.
Note: No impression available.
Plate destroyed.
Zig. No. 21

24. Victimas

Date unknown
Ed. unknown
Size unknown
Drypoint.
Zinc plate.
It is possible that Plate No. 24 and
No. 25 are one and the same.
Zig. No. 22

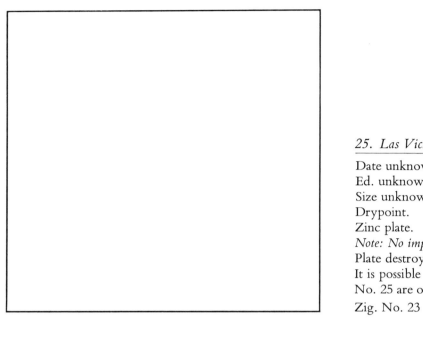

25. *Las Victimas*

Date unknown
Ed. unknown
Size unknown
Drypoint.
Zinc plate.
Note: No impression available.
Plate destroyed.
It is possible that Plate No. 24 and
No. 25 are one and the same.
Zig. No. 23

26. *Papa!*

Date unknown
Ed. unknown
Size unknown
Drypoint.
Zinc plate.
Note: No impression available.
Plate destroyed.
Zig. No. 24

27. Cabeza

1936
Ed. 10
Size unknown
Drypoint.
Zinc plate.
Note: No impression available.
Plate destroyed.
Zig. No. 25

28. Pieta (small)

1936
Ed. 10

	in.	cm.
H.	12-8/16	31.8
W.	10-3/16	25.9

Drypoint.
Zinc plate.
Note: This impression was printed in green ink on a warm, gray paper.
Plate destroyed.
Zig. No. 26

29. *Velorio*

1936
Ed. unknown
Size unknown
Engraving.
Zinc plate.
Note: No impression available.
Plate destroyed.
Zig. No. 27

30. *Cena*

1937
Ed. 10

	in.	cm.
H.	11- 3/16	28.5
W.	12-15/16	32.8

Etching.
Printed in black.
Zinc plate.
Plate destroyed.
Zig. No. 28

31. Carnaval

1936

Ed. 10

	in.	cm.
H.	17-7/16	44.4
W.	12-4/16	31.1

Linoleum cut.

Printed in black on newspaper. The type on the newspaper makes a texture and also a gray.

Block destroyed.

Zig. No. 30

32. Burritos

1937

Ed. 15

	in.	cm.
H.	17	43.2
W.	22-3/16	56.4

Linoleum cut.

Printed in black. This impression was printed on heavy, manila–colored paper.

Block destroyed.

Zig. No. 31

68

33. *Sequía*
1937
Ed. 10

	in.	cm.
H.	16-14/16	42.9
W.	16-13/16	42.7

Linoleum cut.
Printed in black.
Note: This impression was printed on manila-colored paper.
Block destroyed.
Zig. No. 32

34. *Tucumán*
1937
Ed. 8

	in.	cm.
H.	20-12/16	52.8
W.	15-14/16	40.2

Drypoint.
Printed in black on manila-colored paper.
Zinc plate.
Plate destroyed.
Zig. No. 33

35. *El Molino*
1937
Ed. 10

	in.	*cm.*
H.	12	30.5
W.	15-1/4	38.7

Zincografia
Relief etching on zinc.
Note: No impression available.
Plate destroyed.
Zig. No. 34

36. *Changos*
1937
Ed. 25

	in.	*cm.*
H.	15- 7/16	39.2
W.	19-10/16	49.9

Etching on zinc. Printed in black.
Plate destroyed.
Zig. No. 35

37. Changos y Burritos

1937

Ed. 15

	in.	*cm.*
H.	20-14/16	53.1
W.	26-12/16	67.9

Etching; may be touches of drypoint.

Zinc plate.

Plate destroyed.

Zig. No. 36

38. Maternidad

1937

Ed. 5

	in.	*cm.*
H.	22- 4/16	56.6
W.	16-15/16	43.0

Drypoint.

Printed in blueish-black on beige-colored paper.

Zinc plate.

Plate destroyed.

Zig. No. 40

39. Maternidad

Date unknown

Ed. 1

Size unknown

Color trial experiment.

Note: No impression available.

Zig. No. 41

40. Figura

1938

Ed. 15(?)

	in.	cm.
H.	14–14/16	37.7
W.	11–10/16	29.6

Etching; signs of burnishing.

Irregular–shaped plate.

Zinc plate.

Note: This impression was printed with orange ink.

Plate destroyed.

Zig. No. 37

41. *Anunciación*

1938
Ed. 10
Size unknown
Drypoint.
Zinc plate.
Plate destroyed.
Zig. No. 38

42. *Canción de Cuna*

1939
Ed. 10

	in.	cm.
H.	14-1/4	36.7
W.	20-7/8	54.8

Drypoint.
Burin. One plate printed twice, first in sienna, second in Prussian blue.

Copper plate.

Note: Inspired by the cradle song, Los Cinco Burritos *by Javier Villafañe; made for William*

Lasansky. *The New York Public Library has the only impression of the last state in the United States. The only other known impression of this print in the United States is a working proof which is in the collection of William Lasansky.*

Plate destroyed.

Zig. No. 42

(Courtesy of: *Prints Division The New York Public Library Astor, Lenox and Tilden Foundations*)

43. Estudio para un Retrato (Lady with Flower)

1940
Ed. 10

	in.	cm.
H.	18-5/16	46.5
W.	12-8/16	31.7

Drypoint.

Plate printed twice, first in sienna, second in black.

Zinc plate.

Plate destroyed.

Zig. No. 43

44. Un Romance Sonámbulo

1940
Ed. 10

	in.	cm.
H.	20-11/16	52.5
W.	12- 6/16	31.5

Drypoint.

Irregular-shaped plate. Plate printed twice, first in sienna, second in black.

Zinc plate.

Note: Inspired by a poem by Garcia Lorca.

Plate destroyed.

Zig. No. 45

45. *Emilia*
1940
Ed. 10(?)
Size unknown
Drypoint.
Zinc plate.
Note: No impression available.
Plate destroyed.
Zig. No. 46

46. *El Presagio*
1940–1941
Ed. 5

	in.	cm.
H.	24-5/16	61.4
W.	16-6/16	41.6

Drypoint.
Plate printed twice, first in sienna, second in black.
Zinc plate.
Note: There is an impression existing printed in sienna ink on the first run followed by a blueish-black ink.
Plate destroyed.
Zig. No. 44

47. *Retrato de Emilia*

1941

Ed. 10

	in.	*cm.*
H.	15-9/16	39.8
W.	12-6/16	31.7

Drypoint.

Printed in sienna.

Zinc plate.

Plate destroyed.

Zig. No. 47

48. *La Rosa y el Espejo*

1941

Ed. 10

	in.	*cm.*
H.	24- 4/16	61.7
W.	16-13/16	42.7

Drypoint.

Plate printed twice, first in sienna, second in black.

Zinc plate.

Plate destroyed.

Zig. No. 48

49. Figura

1942(?)
Ed. 10

	in.	cm.
H.	7-3/4	19.7
W.	11-1/4	28.6

Drypoint.
Zinc plate.
Note: No impression available.
Plate destroyed.
Zig. No. 49

50. Estudio para un Retrato de A.B. (Barral)

1942
Ed. 6

	in.	cm.
H.	10- 2/16	25.8
W.	9-15/16	25.3

Drypoint.
Plate printed twice, first in sienna, second in black, on manila–colored paper.
Zinc plate.
Note: The top of the plate has been rounded.
Plate destroyed.
Zig. No. 50

51. *Mi Hijo y su Reina de Barajas*

1942

Ed. 10

	in.	*cm.*
H.	15- 2/16	38.4
W.	10-12/16	32.1

Drypoint.

Plate printed twice, first in sienna,
second in black.

Zinc plate.

Plate destroyed.

Zig. No. 51

52. *Motivo Sobre al Cancionero*
      de Heine I

1942

Ed. 10

	in.	*cm.*
H.	6-10/16	16.9
W.	4- 9/16	11.6

Drypoint.

Plate printed twice, first in sienna,
second in black.

Zinc plate.

Plate destroyed.

Zig. No. 52

53. *Motivo Sobre al Cancionero*
   de Heine II

1942
Ed. 10

	in.	cm.
H.	6-8/16	16.5
W.	4-9/16	11.5

Drypoint.
Plate printed twice, first in ochre,
second in blue.
Zinc plate.
Plate destroyed.
Zig. No. 53

54. *Motivo Sobre al Cancionero*
   de Heine III

1942
Ed. 10

	in.	cm.
H.	6-12/16	17.2
W.	4-12/16	12.1

Drypoint.
Plate printed twice.
Zinc plate.
Note: No impression available.
Plate destroyed.
Zig. No. 54

55. Estudio para un Auto Retrato

1943
Ed. 10

	in.	cm.
H.	8-9/16	21.8
W.	6-1/16	15.4

Drypoint.
*Plate printed twice, first in sienna,
second in blue on manila-colored paper.*
Zinc plate.
Plate destroyed.
Zig. No. 55

Prints made in United States

56. Caballo

1944
Ed. 25

	in.	cm.
H.	13-6/16	34.0
W.	5-8/16	13.4

Engraving.
Printed in black.
Copper plate.
Zig. No. 56

57. *Doma*

1944

Ed. (first state) 25

Final edition (50) in 1974

	in.	*cm.*
H.	19-13/16	50.4
W.	13-14/16	35.3

Engraving.

Printed in black.

Copper plate.

Zig. No. 57

58. *Caballos en Celo*

1944

Ed. 50

	in.	*cm.*
H.	13-14/16	35.3
W.	19- 9/16	49.7

Engraving.

Printed in black.

Copper plate.

Zig. No. 58

59. El Cid

1944

Ed. 15

	in.	cm.
H.	27-12/16	70.5
W.	21- 5/16	54.1

Lithograph.

Printed in black.
Tusche drawing, impressed textures,
spattering of tusche, grease crayon.

Stone destroyed.

Zig. No. 59

60. Study

1944

Ed.: This is a unique impression.

	in.	cm.
H.	11-14/16	30.1
W.	11-12/16	29.9

Engraving, soft ground, aquatint,
gouged-out white areas,
burnishing, scraping.
Plate printed twice, first in color,
second in black.

Brass plate.

Not listed in Zigrosser catalogue.

61. Griffanage

1944
Ed. 25

	in.	cm.
H.	12	30.5
W.	8-14/16	22.6

Colors stenciled onto paper. One copper plate printed twice. First run printed with purplish-violet ink, second run printed in black. Engraving, gouged-out white areas, soft ground, grease ground.
Copper plate.
Zig. No. 63

62. La Mariposa

1944
Ed. 50

	in.	cm.
H.	4-15/16	12.5
W.	7-15/16 ·	20.1

Engraving, aquatint, soft ground, etching. One master plate.
Zig. No. 66

62A. La Mariposa

Color impression.
Two plates: one color plate, one copper master plate.

63. La Lagrima

1945

Ed. 50

	in.	cm.
H.	8-14/16	22.6
W.	11-14/16	30.3

Engraving, etching, aquatint, gouged-out white areas, scraping, burnishing.

Two plates: one copper master plate, one color zinc alloy plate.

Zig. No. 60

64. Apocalyptical Space

1945

Ed. 10

	in.	cm.
H.	16	40.5
W.	23-14/16	60.5

Engraving, soft ground, burnishing and scraping, touches of drypoint. Printed in black.

Copper plate.

Plate destroyed.

Note: This impression dated 1944.

Zig. No. 61

65. *Sol y Luna*
1945
Ed. (first state) 35

	in.	cm.
H.	15-13/16	40.1
W.	20-13/16	52.9

Engraving, gouged-out white areas, etching, soft ground, aquatint, scraping, burnishing. Printed in black.
Copper plate.
Zig. No. 62

66. *Bicycle Riders*
1945
Ed. 50

	in.	cm.
H.	26- 9/16	67.6
W.	17-12/16	45.1

Etching.
Copper plate.
Not listed in Zigrosser catalogue.

67. *Self-Portrait*

1945

Ed. 35 (Special edition of 75 in 1973 on color paper.)

	in.	cm.
H.	11–15/16	30.4
W.	9–14/16	25.1

Engraving, signs of scraping, signs of burnishing.

Note: Brass plate, wide bevel; measurements taken from the exterior of the bevel.

Zig. No. 64

68. *Cain*

1945

Ed. (first state) 25

	in.	cm.
H.	24–14/16	60.7
W.	16	40.6

Engraving, etching, soft ground, aquatint, gouged-out white areas.

Copper plate.

Not listed in Zigrosser catalogue.

69. *Object II*

1946

Ed. 35

	in.	cm.
H.	6-15/16	17.7
W.	9	22.9

Engraving, drypoint, aquatint, soft ground.

Copper plate.

Zig. No. 67

70. *Time in Space*

1946

Ed. 35

	in.	cm.
H.	17-15/16	45.5
W.	23-13/16	60.5

Engraving, etching, aquatint, soft ground, extensive burnishing and scraping, large open–bite areas, electric stippler.

Copper plate.

Zig. No. 65

Detail of Plate for *Dachau* (1946). Catalogue number 71.

71. *Dachau*

1946

Ed. 35

	in.	cm.
H.	15-10/16	39.8
W.	23-11/16	60.1

*Plate bitten and worked in multi-levels
(stopped-out areas with deep open
bite) containing engraving,
gouged-out white areas, soft ground,
etching, aquatint, extensive
burnishing and scraping.*

Copper plate.

Zig. No. 68

72. *For an Eye an Eye I*

1946 to 1948
Ed. 50

	in.	cm.
H.	26-5/16	66.8
W.	21-1/16	53.6

*Etching, soft ground, aquatint,
open-bite areas, extensive
scraping and burnishing.*
Copper plate.
Zig. No. 69

73. *For an Eye an Eye II*

1946 to 1948
Ed. 50

	in.	cm.
H.	27– 2/16	68.8
W.	21-10/16	54.9

*Etching, soft ground, aquatint,
gouged–out white areas, electric
stippler, extensive scraping
and burnishing.*
Copper plate.
Zig. No. 70

74. *For an Eye an Eye III*

1946 to 1948
Ed. 50

	in.	cm.
H.	27	68.5
W.	21-8/16	54.6

*Etching, aquatint, open-bite areas,
lift ground, electric stippler, extensive
scraping and burnishing.*
Copper plate.
Zig. No. 71

75. For an Eye an Eye IV

1946 to 1948

Ed. 50

	in.	cm.
H.	26-5/16	66.8
W.	21-1/16	53.6

Etching, engraving, stopped-out open-bite areas, aquatint, electric stippler, extensive scraping and burnishing.

One copper plate.

Zig. No. 72

76. *Spring*

1947

Ed. 50

	in.	cm.
H.	23-12/16	60.4
W.	8-12/16	22.1

Engraving, etching, soft ground, aquatint, large open–bite areas, electric stippler.

Nine copper plates: one master plate printed in black, eight color plates.

Zig. No. 73

77. *Fall*

1947

Ed. 5 (?)

	in.	cm.
H.	23-14/16	16.6
W.	8	21.0

Engraving, aquatint, open–bite areas.

Two copper plates: one color plate, one master plate.

Zig. No. 74

78. *Winter*

1947

Ed. 5

	in.	cm.
H.	24	61.0
W.	8-6/16	21.3

Engraving, etching, soft ground, aquatint, electric stippler, large open–bite areas.

Four copper plates.

Note: All plates contain color in the intaglio areas except for the purple, which is rolled on. Lower right hand corner red area is a cut-out plate which is placed upon the master plate, then printed. This approach is again taken up in Bleeding Heart (1970), *and* Quetzalcoatl (1972).

Zig. No. 75

79. *Black Print*

1947

Ed. Unique print, trial proof.

	in.	cm.
H.	23-12/16	60.3
W.	17-10/16	44.8

Engraving, soft ground, aquatint, etching, open-bite areas, burnishing and scraping.

Note: Two copper plates printed in black ink on black paper; the plates are positioned side by side. One is the master plate of Winter *and the other is the master plate of* Spring *while still in state form.*

Not listed in Zigrosser catalogue.

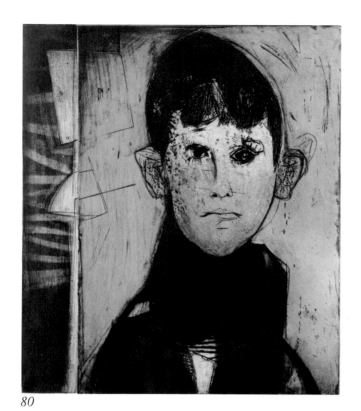

80

80A

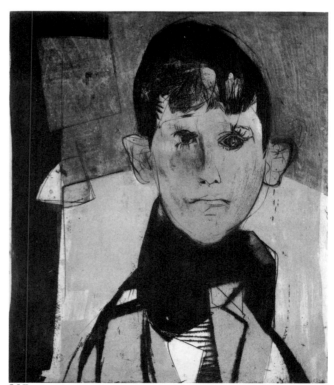

80B

80. My Boy

1947

Ed. 35

	in.	cm.
H.	16-15/16	43.0
W.	14	35.6

Engraving, etching, aquatint, soft ground, open-bite areas, electric stippler, burnishing, extensive scraping.

Five plates: two copper master plates, three copper color plates.

Note: Six states of this print exist to my knowledge.

Zig. No. 76

(From the private collection of Bodine Lamont)

80A. State

Same size.

One copper master plate, three copper color plates.

Note: The face is flesh-colored and the body is pink. The background is a blue-green on the right side, and a brownish-red under the abstract forms on the left.

80B. State

Same size.

One copper master plate, three copper color plates.

Note: The face is flesh-colored and the body is pink. The background is green on the top and lemon-yellow green on the bottom.

<u>*81. My Wife*</u>

1947

Ed. 35

Color plates:

	in.	*cm.*
H.	21-4/16	58.3
W.	16-9/16	42.2

Master plates:

	in.	*cm.*
H.	17-15/16	45.6
W.	14-14/16	37.7

Engraving, etching, soft ground, water ground, aquatint, burnishing and scraping.

Six copper plates: five color plates, one master plate.

Note: This plate was used for the print My Wife and Thomas *(1959).*

Zig. No. 77

82. Self-Portrait

1948
Ed. 50

	in.	cm.
H.	23-15/16	60.8
W.	15-13/16	40.2

*Engraving, etching, soft ground,
aquatint, open-bite areas,
scraping and burnishing.*

*Three plates: two zinc color plates,
one copper master plate.*

Zig. No. 78

82A. State

Same size.
Note: This is a state without glasses.

83. *Pieta*

1948

Ed. 35

	in.	cm.
H.	19-4/16	49.0
W.	28	71.1

Engraving, etching, soft ground, aquatint, lift ground, grease ground, electric stippler, extensive scraping and burnishing.

Nine plates: eight zinc color plates, one copper master plate.

Note: Master plate is printed twice in black.

Zig. No. 79

84. *El Pajaro*

1948

Ed. 50

	in.	cm.
H.	28-14/16	73.3
W.	22- 5/16	56.6

Engraving, etching, soft ground, aquatint, extensive scraping and burnishing, scorped-out white areas, drypoint, several large open-bite areas, varnish resist.

One copper plate, printed in black.

Zig. No. 80

85. Aitana

1948

Ed. 35

	in.	*cm.*
H.	26-12/16	67.9
W.	11-13/16	30.1

Engraving, etching, soft ground, aquatint, grease ground, electric stippler, drypoint touches.

Five plates: four zinc color plates, one copper master plate.

Zig. No. 81

86. Near East (Pieta)

1948

Ed. 35

	in.	*cm.*
H.	19- 3/16	48.1
W.	23-14/16	60.7

Engraving, etching, aquatint, soft ground, electric stippler, grease ground, deep open-bite areas, burnishing and scraping.

Seven plates: six zinc color plates, one copper master plate printed in black.

Zig. No. 82

87. Self-Portrait

1949

Ed. 25

	in.	cm.
H.	13	33.1
W.	9-14/16	25.1

Engraving, etching, soft ground, scraping and burnishing.

Copper plate.

Not listed in Zigrosser catalogue.

88. Self-Portrait (*In frame*)

1950

Ed. 50

Color plates: Master plate:

	in.	cm.		in.	cm.
H.	21-1/16	53.4	H.	15- 4/16	38.8
W.	19	48.4	W.	16-13/16	42.8

Engraving, etching, aquatint, electric stippler, scraping and burnishing.

Three plates: two zinc color plates, one copper master printed twice, first in yellow ochre, second in black.

Zig. No. 83

88A. State

	in.	cm.
H.	15-1/2	38.7
W.	16-3/4	42.6

One copper plate. Printed in black.

89. State
Same size as *89A*.

89A. Bodas de Sangre
1951
Ed. 50

	in.	cm.
H.	20- 6/16	51.7
W.	28-11/16	73.0

Engraving, etching, gouged-out white areas, aquatint, soft ground, resists, lift ground, electric stippler, grease ground, extensive scraping and burnishing.

Nine plates: one copper master, eight zinc color plates.

Note: Inspired by Garcia Lorca.

Zig. No. 84

90. Firebird

1952–1953

Ed. 50

	in.	cm.
H.	21- 5/16	54.1
W.	33-15/16	86.2

Engraving, etching, soft ground, aquatint, electric stippler, gouged-out white areas, scraping and burnishing.

Copper plate.

Zig. No. 85

91. *Boy*

1954

Ed. 50

	in.	cm.
H.	24	50.9
W.	13-6/16	33.9

Engraving, soft ground, aquatint, grease ground (could be water ground), open-bite areas, electric stippler, scraping and burnishing.

Four plates: three zinc color plates, one copper master plate.

Zig. No. 86

92. *Sagittarius*

1955

Ed. 50

	in.	cm.
H.	21-6/16	52.4
W.	35-6/16	89.8

Engraving, etching, soft ground, aquatint, lift ground or aquatinted stopped-out areas, electric stippler, scraping and burnishing.

Copper plate.

Note: Plate is slightly shaped on three sides.

Zig. No. 87

93. The Vision

1956

Ed. 50

	in.	cm.
H.	23-13/16	60.4
W.	21-10/16	55.0

Etching, engraving, aquatint, soft ground, electric stippler, scraping and burnishing.

One copper plate printed twice, first in yellow ochre, second in black.

Zig. No. 88

94. España

1956

Ed. 50

	in.	cm.
H.	31-14/16	80.9
W.	20-12/16	52.7

Etching, engraving, aquatint, soft ground, scraping and burnishing.

One copper plate printed twice, first in yellow ochre, second in black.

Zig. No. 89

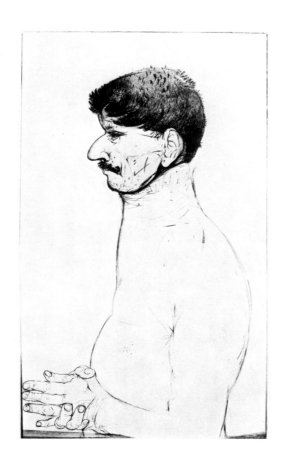

95. Self-Portrait

1957

Ed. 50

	in.	*cm.*
H.	35-12/16	91.0
W.	20-10/16	52.4

Engraving, electric stippler,
scraping and burnishing.

One magnesium plate printed twice,
first in yellow ochre, second in black.

Zig. No. 90

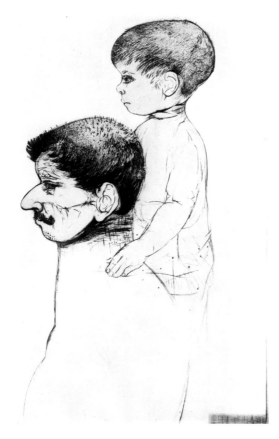

96. Father and Son

1958

Ed. 50

	in.	*cm.*
H.	35-13/16	91.0
W.	20-15/16	53.1

Engraving (plus multi-burin),
scraping, electric stippler.

One magnesium plate printed twice,
first in yellow ochre, second in black.

Zig. No. 91

97. *Nacimiento en Cardiel*

1958

Ed. 50

	in.	cm.
H.	21-3/16	53.9
W.	32-4/16	81.9

Etching, drypoint, soft ground, aquatint, electric stippler, shallow surface bite, scraping and burnishing.

One copper plate printed twice, first in yellow ochre, second in black.

Zig. No. 92

<u>*98. My Son Leonardo*</u>

1959

Ed. (first state) 50

	in.	cm.
H.	25-6/16	64.5
W.	16-6/16	41.6

Engraving, etching, aquatint, soft ground, electric stippler, scraping and burnishing.

Four plates: two zinc color plates, two copper master plates.

Zig. No. 93

99. Self-Portrait

1959

Ed. 50

	in.	cm.
H.	66-14/16	169.9
W.	20- 9/16	52.3

Etching, aquatint, soft ground,
open-bite, water ground,
electric stippler.

Three plates: one zinc color plate,
two master plates.

Zig. No. 94

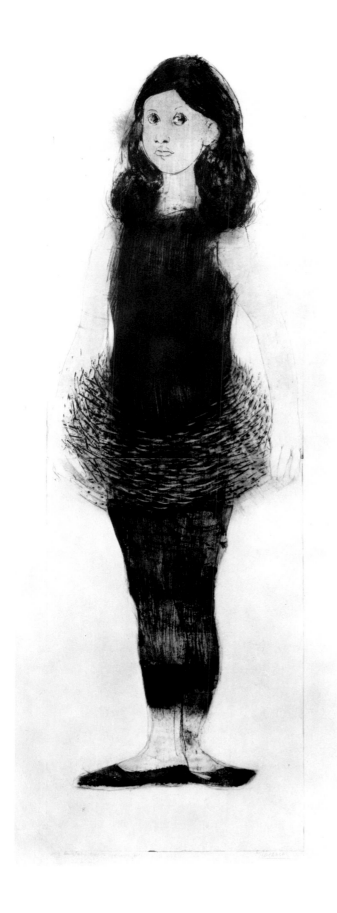

100. My Daughter Maria Jimena

1959

Ed. 50

	in.	*cm.*
H.	58-13/16	174.7
W.	20- 9/16	52.2

Engraving, etching, soft ground, aquatint, electric stippler.

Five plates: two zinc alloy color plates, three copper master plates.

Zig. No. 95

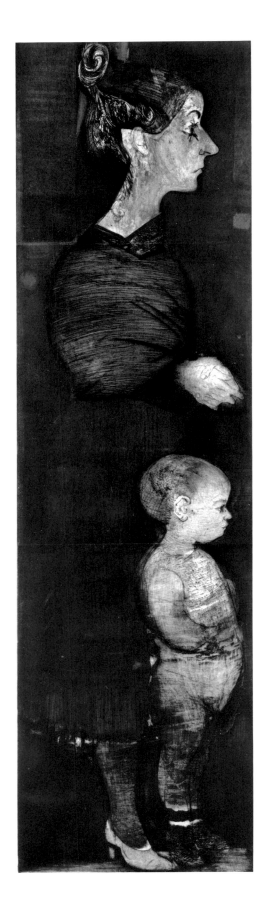

101. My Wife and Thomas

1959
Ed. 50

	in.	cm.
H.	74-5/16	188.8
W.	20	50.8

Engraving, etching, water ground, aquatint, grease ground, soft ground, electric stippler, scraping and burnishing.
Nine plates: five zinc alloy color plates, four copper master plates.
Zig. No. 96
(*My Wife and Thomas* is the last listed print in the Zigrosser catalogue. The catalogue lists through 1959.)

102. Study of Jimena

1961
Ed. 70

	in.	cm.
H.	17-12/16	45.0
W.	16- 2/16	40.9

Engraving, etching, soft ground, water ground, aquatint.
Three plates: two zinc color plates, one copper master plate.

103. La Jimena

1960 or 1961

Ed. 50

	in.	cm.
H.	65- 9/16	166.6
W.	18-14/16	48.0

Engraving, etching, soft ground, drypoint, electric stippler, scraping and burnishing.

Four plates: one color plate, three copper master plates.

104. Portrait of an Artist

1961

Ed.: First, 50; Second, 50

	in.	cm.
H.	20- 4/16	51.4
W.	16-15/16	43.0

Engraving, etching, soft ground, drypoint, electric stippler.

Three plates: two zinc alloy color plates, one copper master plate.

105. El Maestro

1962

Ed. 70

	in.	cm.
H.	15	38.1
W.	15	38.1

Engraving, soft ground, etching,
drypoint, grease ground, aquatint.

Three plates: two zinc color plates,
one copper master plate.

106. Portrait of a Poet

(Rocio Aitana) [Small]

1962

Ed. 35

Print size:

	in.	cm.
H.	15-1/16	39.5
W.	16	40.6

Master plate size:

	in.	cm.
H.	14-14/16	37.8
W.	16	40.6

Engraving, etching, soft ground,
water ground, drypoint,
electric stippler.

Three plates: two zinc color plates,
one copper master plate.

107. *Portrait of a Poet*

(*Rocio Aitana*)

1962

Ed. 10

Print size:

	in.	cm.
H.	15- 8/16	39.4
W.	20-14/16	53.0

Master plate size:

	in.	cm.
H.	14-14/16	37.8
W.	15-14/16	40.4

*Engraving, etching, drypoint, soft
ground, water ground, electric stippler.*

*Three plates: two zinc color plates,
one copper master plate.*

*Note: Plate belongs to life-size
figure unfinished.*

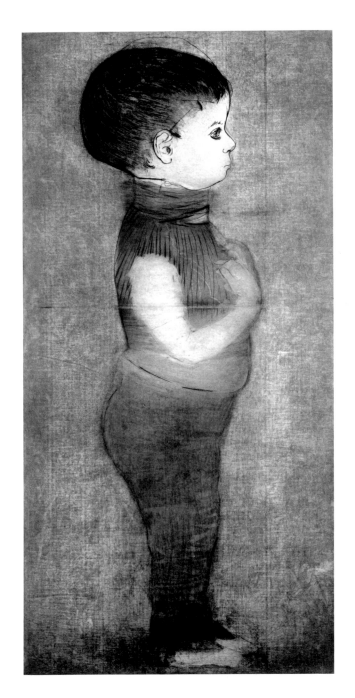

108. Thomas

1962

Ed. 50

	in.	cm.
H.	41-13/16	106.1
W.	19	48.2

Engraving, etching, soft ground, aquatint, electric stippler.

Five plates: three zinc alloy color plates, two copper master plates.

109. State

Same size as *109A.*

Engraving.

Three master (two zinc, one copper) plates, one galvanized steel color plate.

109A. Luis Felipe

1963

Ed. 50

	in.	cm.
H.	49-14/16	126.7
W.	21	53.3

Engraving, etching, soft ground, aquatint, electric stippler, drypoint, scraping.

Six plates: three zinc alloy color plates, three master (two zinc, one copper) plates.

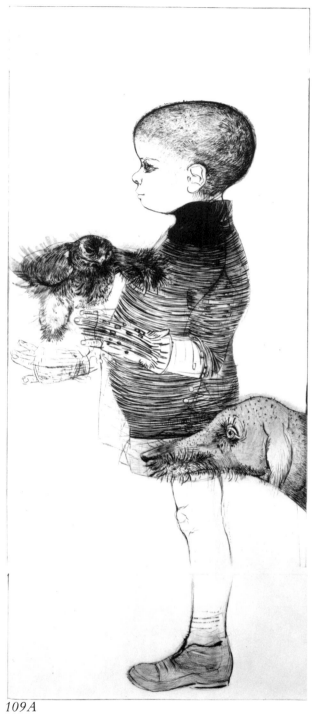

109A

109

110A

110

110B

110. State: Full-length print

Same size as *110B*.
Color note: The figure is printed in black.

110A. State: head

	in.	cm.
H.	14-15/16	37.9
W.	13- 1/2	34.3

110B. Boy with Cat

1964
Ed. 50

	in.	cm.
H.	52-12/16	134.0
W.	23-14/16	60.8

Engraving, etching, soft ground, drypoint, electric stippler, aquatint, scraping and burnishing.
Five plates: two color plates, three master plates.

111. El Cardenal

1964
Ed. 50

	in.	cm.
H.	28-14/16	73.3
W.	18- 5/16	46.5

Engraving, etching, drypoint, soft ground resist, water ground or grease ground, aquatint, electric stippler.

Three plates: two zinc alloy color plates, one copper master plate.

112. Pope

1965
Ed. 20

	in.	cm.
H.	22- 3/4	56.3
W.	17-15/16	45.7

Engraving, etching, drypoint, aquatint, grease ground, electric stippler, scraping and burnishing.

Three plates: two color plates (one zinc and one copper), one copper master plate.

113. *Portrait of a Young Artist*

1965
Ed. 70

	in.	cm.
H.	19- 6/16	49.3
W.	17-14/16	45.4

Engraving (touches), etching, aquatint, soft ground, electric stippler.
Two plates: one zinc color plate, one copper master plate.

114. *Head of a Young Girl*
    (Amana Girl Head)

1965
State

	in.	cm.
H.	18	45.7
W.	16	40.6

Engraving, etching, drypoint, soft ground, aquatint.
Three plates: two zinc color plates, one copper master plate.

115

116

117

115. Amana Girl (Life-size)

1965

Ed. 35

	in.	cm.
H.	46-12/16	118.7
W.	21-15/16	55.7

Engraving, etching, soft ground, electric stippler, scraping and burnishing.

Five plates: three color plates zinc-galvanized steel, two copper master plates.

Color note: pink hat and apron, orange background, two bows on braids, one white, one red.

116. Amana Girl (Life-size)

1965

Ed. 35

	in.	cm.
H.	46-12/16	118.7
W.	21-15/16	55.7

Engraving, etching, soft ground, electric stippler, scraping and burnishing.

Four plates: two zinc-galvanized steel color plates, two copper master plates.

Color note: light blue hat and apron, flesh-colored background.

117. Woman with Lute

1965

Ed. 50

	in.	cm.
H.	74-11/16	189.7
W.	23-13/16	60.5

Engraving, etching, soft ground, sandpaper, aquatint, electric stippler, scraping and burnishing.

Six plates: two zinc-galvanized steel color plates, four copper master plates.

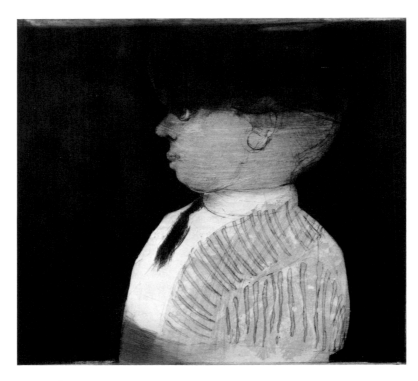

118. El Mozo

1966

Ed. 70

	in.	cm.
H.	15-15/16	40.5
W.	17-13/16	45.2

Engraving, etching, soft ground,
open-bite, drypoint, resist ground.
Three plates: two zinc color plates,
one copper master plate.

119. Pope and Cardinal

1966

Ed. 50

	in.	*cm.*
H.	74–8/16	189.2
W.	32–5/16	82.2

Engraving, etching, drypoint, soft ground, embossing, electric stippler, water ground, grease ground, scraping and burnishing.

Ten assembled shaped copper, zinc-galvanized steel plates.

120

121

122

120. Amana Girl in Red with Dog

1967

Working trial proof

	in.	cm.
H.	47- 2/16	119.7
W.	21-15/16	55.8

Engraving, etching, soft ground, electric stippler, scraping and burnishing.

Four plates: two zinc-galvanized steel color plates, two copper master plates.

Note: This is a reworking of Amana Girl *(Life-size).*

Note on color: red body, green hat, brown shoes, ochre background. Short leg stool printed in red.

121. Amana Girl in Red Winter Coat

1967

Ed. 70

	in.	cm.
H.	47- 5/16	120.0
W.	21-15/16	55.8

Engraving, etching, aquatint, soft ground, electric stippler, scraping and burnishing.

Five plates: two zinc-galvanized color plates, three copper master plates.

Note: Reworking on front of figure. The chair has been extended in length, texture added on floor. Scraping and burnishing on body which now denotes form of an arm.

Color change: cap is red, the shoes green.

122. Amana Girl in Black Winter Coat

1967

Ed. 70

	in.	cm.
H.	47	119.4
W.	21-15/16	55.8

Engraving, etching, electric stippler, soft ground, aquatint, drypoint, relief printing, scraping and burnishing, photoengraving.

Six plates: two intaglio zinc-galvanized steel color plates, one relief color plate, three copper master plates.

Note: Figure is reworked. In addition is a photoengraved plate which is of Dürer's Rhinocerus *printed in relief. Dog now has color on his neck. Chair has been shortened and the girl now sits on a pillow.*

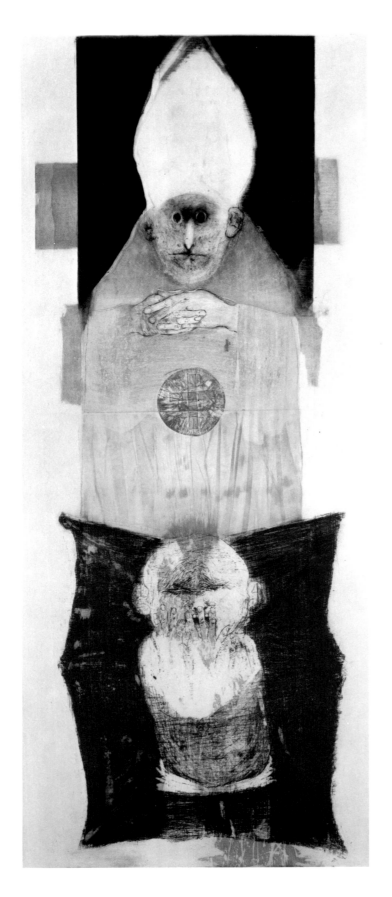

123. Pope and Crying Boy

1967
Ed. 50

	in.	cm.
H.	65-12/16	167.0
W.	23-12/16	60.3

Etching, soft ground, aquatint, embossment, drypoint, electric stippler, grease ground.
Nine assembled shaped copper, zinc-galvanized steel plates.
Note: Head is from Pope *and* Pope and Cardinal.

124. Amish Boy

1967
Ed. 70

	in.	cm.
H.	27	68.5
W.	17-14/16	45.4

Etching, engraving, drypoint, soft ground, aquatint, electric stippler.
Four plates: three zinc alloy color plates, one copper master plate.

125. Lady in Blue

1967

Ed. 50

	in.	cm.
H.	75- 9/16	192.1
W.	25-10/16	65.3

*Engraving, etching, soft ground,
aquatint, drypoint, electric stippler.*

*Three plates: two color plates, one
copper master plate which is the
length of the print.*

126. The Artist Approaching
Middle Age

1968

Ed. 70

	in.	cm.
H.	19-12/16	50.1
W.	17-14/16	45.5

*Engraving, etching, soft ground.
Three plates: two zinc alloy color
plates, one copper master plate.*

127. *Thomas with Cap*

1968

Color trial proof

	in.	cm.
H.	29-2/16	74.0
W.	18-6/16	46.6

Engraving, etching, soft ground, reverse soft ground, electric stippler, scraping and burnishing.

Three plates: two zinc alloy color plates, one copper master plate.

128. *Young Lady*

1968

Ed. 70

	in.	cm.
H.	28-10/16	72.7
W.	18- 6/16	46.7

Engraving, etching, soft ground, aquatint, electric stippler, water ground, scraping and burnishing.

Four plates: three zinc alloy color plates, one copper master plate.

Note: Reworking of plate of Thomas with Cap.

129. Little Girl

1968
Ed. 70

	in.	cm.
H.	15- 7/16	39.2
W.	13-13/16	35.2

*Etching, soft ground, drypoint,
grease ground, electric stippler,
scraping and burnishing.*

*Three plates: two zinc alloy color
plates, one copper master plate.*

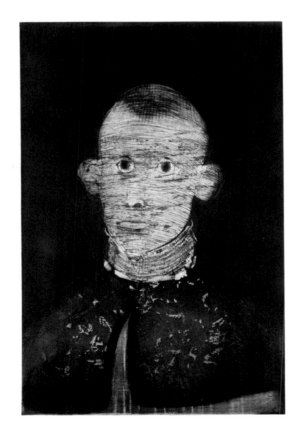

130. Gregorian Chanter

1968
Ed. 70

	in.	cm.
H.	29	73.8
W.	18-5/16	46.4

*Engraving, etching, soft ground,
aquatint, touches of drypoint,
electric stippler.*

*Three plates: two zinc-galvanized
steel color plates, one copper
master plate.*

Note: Contains one plate from
Thomas with Cap *which was
reworked and became* Young Lady.

*This head belongs to a life-size
plate not finished.*

131. Old Lady in Black with Hands on Face

1969

Trial Proof

	in.	cm.
H.	20-8/16	52.1
W.	16-5/16	41.6

Engraving, drypoint, aquatint, soft ground, scraping and burnishing.

Three plates: one copper master plate, two zinc alloy color plates, one of which is printed in black.

Note: There are no plate marks on the width of the print; dimensions are given from the widest part of the printed image.

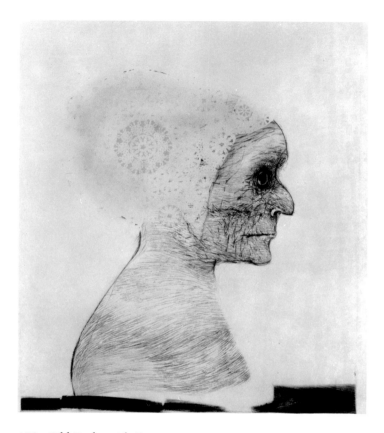

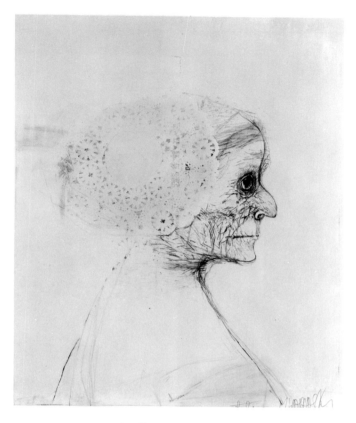

132. Old Lady with Bonnet

1969

Ed. 70

	in.	*cm.*
H.	22- 1/16	56.0
W.	17-11/16	45.0

Etching, drypoint, embossment.

Three plates: two zinc alloy color plates, one copper master plate.

132A. Drawing and collage on state of print

133. Oriental Image

1969

Ed. 50

	in.	cm.
H.	76-13/16	195.1
W.	25-13/16	65.7

Etching, soft ground, drypoint, electric stippler, scraping and burnishing, embossment.

Five plates: three zinc alloy, galvanized steel color plates, two copper master plates.

133

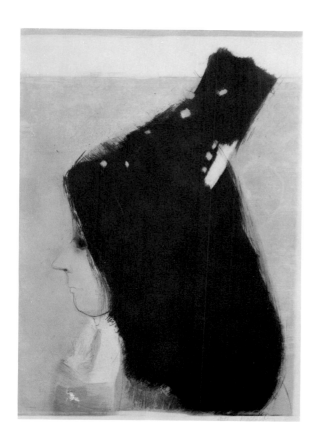

133A. State: Head

Size of printed image:

	in.	cm.
H.	23-13/16	60.7
W.	16- 6/16	41.7

133B. State: Head

Size of printed image:

	in.	cm.
H.	23-6/16	59.3
W.	16-6/16	41.7

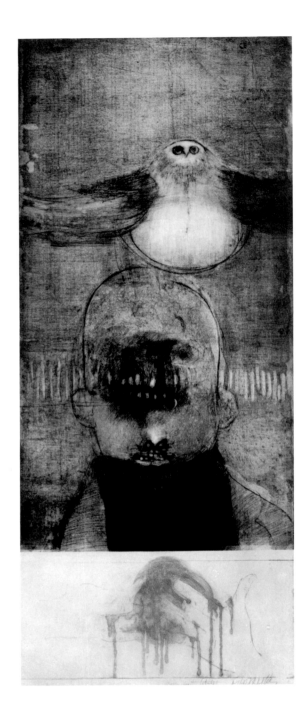

134. *State*

	in.	cm.
H.	43–14/16	111.5
W.	18	45.8

134A. Bleeding Heart

1970

Ed. 70

	in.	cm.
H.	47-9/16	120.9
W.	22-4/16	56.4

Engraving, etching, soft ground, drypoint, aquatint, open–bite areas, water ground, electric stippler, embossment, scraping and burnishing.

Twenty-one assembled shaped copper, zinc alloy, galvanized steel plates.

135. State

Same size as 135C.
Color note: brown body, red cap, and white hair.

135A. State

Same size as 135C.
Color note: blue body, green hair, and green and red-orange cap.

135B. State
Same size as *135C*.

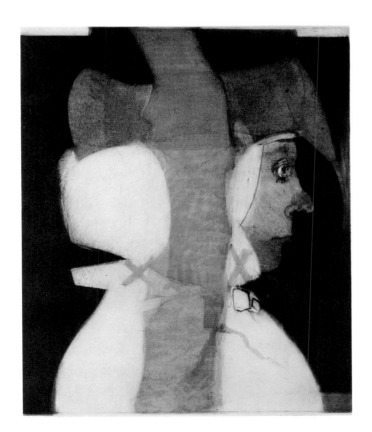

135C. Profile with Red Band
1970
Ed. 70

	in.	cm.
H.	19-14/16	50.5
W.	16- 4/16	41.3

Engraving, etching, drypoint, aquatint, soft ground with leaf resist, electric stippler, scraping and burnishing.

Three plates: two zinc alloy color plates, one copper master plate.

Note: This plate has gone through an extensive amount of working proofs, some of which are very beautiful in their subtle color relationships.

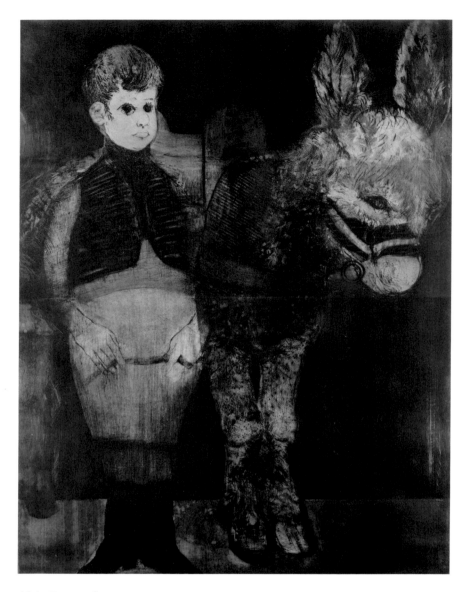

136. Boy with Burro

1960–1971

Ed. 70

	in.	cm.
H.	47-12/16	121.2
W.	34-13/16	88.5

Engraving, etching, soft ground,
electric stippler, drypoint, aquatint,
open-bite areas, scraping
and burnishing.

Four plates: two zinc alloy color
plates, two copper master plates.

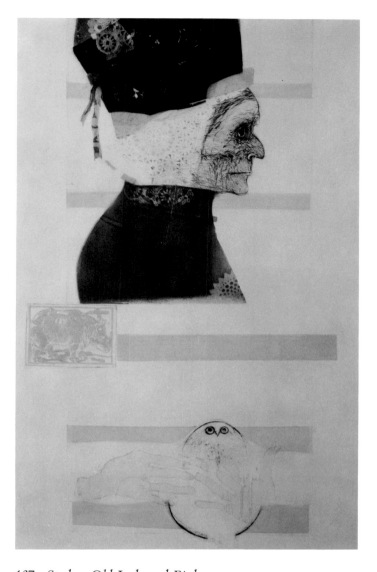 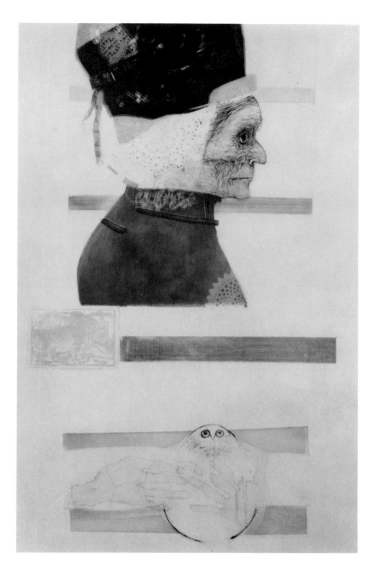

137. *Study—Old Lady and Bird*

1971

Working trial proof

	in.	*cm.*
H.	40-4/16	102.2
W.	22-7/16	57.1

Engraving, etching, soft ground, electric stippler, drypoint, open-bite areas (could be lift ground), embossment, scraping and burnishing, photoengraving.

Ten assembled copper, zinc alloy, galvanized steel shaped plates.

Note: Dürer's Rhinocerus *plate from* Seated Girl in Black with Dog *is used here; this time it is printed in intaglio.*

Color note: blueish-gray bust of figure. Yellow, green, and blue bands of color.

138. *Study—Old Lady and Bird*

1971

Working trial proof.

	in.	*cm.*
H.	40- 4/16	102.2
W.	22-11/16	57.7

Engraving, etching, soft ground, electric stippler, drypoint, open-bite areas (could be lift ground), embossment, scraping and burnishing.

Ten assembled copper, zinc alloy, galvanized steel shaped plates.

Color note: brown bust of figure; yellow bands of color.

139. Quetzalcoatl

1972

Ed. 50

	in.	cm.
H.	75-11/16	192.3
W.	33- 8/16	85.2

Engraving, etching, drypoint, soft ground, reverse soft ground, electric stippler, aquatint, lift ground, scraping and burnishing.

Fifty-four plates: one galvanized color master plate; forty-five copper, zinc alloy, galvanized steel assembled shaped plates; eight copper master plates.

140. *State*

1961

	in.	cm.
H.	43	109.2
W.	18	45.8

140A. *Young Nahua Dancer*

1961–1973

Ed. 70

	in.	cm.
H.	48- 4/16	122.6
W.	26-14/16	68.3

*Mezzotint, etching, soft ground,
drypoint, reverse soft ground,
engraving, electric stippler, scraping
and burnishing.*

*Forty-six plates: one steel color
master plate; forty-one color, copper,
zinc alloy, galvanized steel assembled
plates; three master plates, two
copper, one zinc alloy; one dry
printing shaped plate.*

Mauricio Lasansky in his Iowa City studio (1966).

Mauricio Lasansky

1914
Born October 12, 1914, in Buenos Aires, Argentina

1933
Attended Superior School of Fine Arts, Argentina

1936
*Director of the Free Fine Arts School, Villa Maria,
Cordoba, Argentina*

1937
Married Emilia Barragan December 16, 1937

1938
Guillermo Abraham Lasansky born October 15, 1938

1939
Director of the Taller Manualidades, Cordoba, Argentina

1942
Rocio Aitana Lasansky born January 4, 1942

1943
Received a Guggenheim Fellowship to come to the United States

1944
Guggenheim Fellowship Renewed

1945
*Visiting Lecturer to create a Graphic Arts Department at
The University of Iowa, Iowa City*

1946
Assistant Professor of Art at The University of Iowa

1946
Leonardo Lasansky born March 29, 1946

1947
Associate Professor of Art at The University of Iowa

1947
Maria Jimena Lasansky born October 5, 1947

1948
Professor of Art at The University of Iowa

1952
Became an American citizen

1953–54
*Received Guggenheim Fellowship for one year in Spain
and France*

1954
One-man show, Museo de Arte Contemporaneo, Madrid, Spain

1954
Luis Phillip Lasansky born December 10, 1954

1954
One-man show, Centro Catalan, Barcelona, Spain

1955
*Invitational Exhibition, "Contemporary American Art,"
Museum of Modern Art, Paris*

1955
*Invitational Exhibition, "International Exposition of
Contemporary Gravure," Ljubljana, Yugoslavia*

1955
*Invitational Exhibition, "III Bienal Hispanoamericana de
Arte," Barcelona, Spain*

1956
*Invitational Exhibition, "Contemporary American
Printmakers," University of Illinois (Smithsonian Institute
Traveling Show)*

1956
*Invitational Exhibition, "20 American Printmakers,"
Michigan State University, East Lansing*

1957
*Eyre Medal: Pennsylvania Academy of The Fine Arts
Annual Exhibition*

1957
Charles M. Lea Prize: Philadelphia Print Club Exhibition

1957
*Invitational Exhibition, "10 Contemporary Printmakers,"
Bloomington-Normal Art Association, Bloomington, Illinois*

1957
Invitational Exhibition, 4th International Bordighera Biennale, Italy

1957
Invitational Exhibition, "International Exposition of Contemporary Gravure," Ljubljana, Yugoslavia

1957
Retrospective Exhibition, The University of Iowa, Iowa City

1957
Thomas Lasansky born August 31, 1957

1958
Posada Award: Invitational Exhibition, "Primera Exposition Bienal Interamericana de Pintura y Grabado en Mexico," Mexico City, Mexico

1958
Purchase Prize: Silvermine Guild 2nd National Print Exhibition, New Canaan, Connecticut

1958
Purchase Prize: Pasadena Art Museum National Print Exhibition, Pasadena, California

1958
Purchase Prize: Brooklyn Museum 11th National Print Exhibition, Brooklyn, New York

1959
Awarded Honorary Doctor of Arts Degree by Iowa Wesleyan College, Mount Pleasant, Iowa

1959
One-man show: "Intaglios," Latin American Traveling Show, traveling under the auspices of the United States Information Agency for a three-year period

1959
Invitational Exhibition, "100 American Works on Paper," Institute of Contemporary Art, Boston; traveling in Europe for one year

1959
Invitational Exhibition, "Incisori Americani Contemporanei." Contemporary American Prints, organized by the Brooklyn Museum, Brooklyn, New York, to travel in Europe

1960
Awarded Retrospective Exhibition by Ford Foundation; traveling show under the auspices of the American Federation of Arts (1960–1962)

1960
Invitational Exhibition, 2nd International Biennial, Palace of Fine Arts, Mexico City, Mexico

1961
One-man shows: Los Angeles County Museum, Los Angeles, California; Brooklyn Museum, Brooklyn, New York; School of Art, Syracuse University, Syracuse, New York; Seattle Art Museum, Seattle, Washington

1961
Invited small one-man show, 156th Annual Exhibition Pennsylvania Academy of The Fine Arts, Philadelphia, Pennsylvania

1962
Purchase Awards: Pasadena Art Museum, Pasadena, California; 12th Annual Mid-America, Nelson Gallery, Kansas City, Missouri

1962
Charles M. Lea Prize: The Print Club, Philadelphia, Pennsylvania

1963
Purchase Awards: 2nd National Invitational Print Exhibition Otis Art Institute, Los Angeles County, Los Angeles, California

1963
Purchase Award: 19th National Exhibition of Prints, Library of Congress, Washington, D.C.

1964
Invitational Exhibition, Sixth Exposition Internationale de Gravure, Ljubljana, Yugoslavia

1964–65
New York World's Fair

1965
Research Professorship, The University of Iowa

1965
Guggenheim Fellowship to Spain and Latin America

1965
*Awarded Accademico Onorario of the classe di Incisione from
the Accademia Delle Arti del Designo, Florence, Italy*
1965
Lucas Lecturer, Carleton College, Northfield, Minnesota
1965
*Named to the Fine Arts Jury of the John Simon Guggenheim
Memorial Foundation*
1966
*Invitational Exhibition, First International Biennial of Prints,
Kracow, Poland*
1967
*Virgil M. Hancher Distinguished Professor of Art, The
University of Iowa*
1967
*Invitational Exhibition, Seventh International Exhibition
of Prints, Ljubljana, Yugoslavia*
1967
*One-man show: "Mauricio Lasansky: Selections from Thirty
Years of Printmaking," Iowa State University, Ames, Iowa*
1968
*Invitational Exhibition, Second International Biennial of Prints,
Kracow, Poland*
1968
*Invitational Exhibitions: "American Prints," National
Academy of Fine Arts, Amsterdam, Holland, and
"25 American Artists," The Hague, Holland*
1969
*Awarded Honorary Doctorate of Fine Arts Degree by Pacific
Lutheran University, Tacoma, Washington*
1969
*One-man show: "The Nazi Drawings," Palace of Fine Arts,
Mexico City, Mexico*
1969
*Invitational Exhibition, 1st British International Print Show,
Bradford City, England*
1970
Elected to Board of Directors of the College Art Association
1970
Research Professorship 1971–72, The University of Iowa

1970
*One-man show: "The Nazi Drawings," The University
of Iowa Museum of Art*
1970
*Invitational Exhibitions: 35th Biennial Art Exhibition in
Venice, Italy, and the 2nd International Biennial of
Graphic Art in Florence, Italy*
1971
*Invitational Exhibitions: 1st International Biennial of
Graphic Arts, Honolulu, Hawaii; "Graphic der Welt,"
Albertina Museum, Vienna; "International Biennial of Prints
and Drawings," Cali, Colombia; "Biennial of the Moderna
Galeria," Ljubljana, Yugoslavia*
1972
One-man show, Dickinson College, Carlisle, Pennsylvania
1972
*Invitational Exhibition, "American Prints: '72," Ames, Iowa
Dedicated to Prof. Lasansky's 27 years of teaching at
The University of Iowa*
1972
*Invitational Exhibitions: "3rd Biennial of Graphic Art,"
Palazzo Strozzi in Florence, Italy; 2nd San Juan Biennial in
Puerto Rico; International Prints Biennale in Fredrikstad,
Norway*
1973
*Invitational Exhibitions: "2nd American Biennial of Graphic
Arts, Cali, Colombia; Prints in Exhibition in Colombia,
South America; "American Prints 1973," Ames, Iowa*
1974
*Invitational Exhibition, "3rd International Biennial
Exhibition," San Juan, Puerto Rico*
1974
*"The Dickinson College Arts Award, 1974–75,"
Dickinson College, Carlisle, Pennsylvania*

Works in Permanent Collections

In Argentina:

Museo de Mendoza
Museo Municipal, Buenos Aires
Museo Municipal, Rio Cuarto
Museo Municipal de Cordoba, Cordoba
Museo Municipal Rosario, Sante Fe
Museo Nacional de Bellas Artes, Buenos Aires
Museo Provincal de Cordoba, Cordoba
Museo Provincal, La Plata, Buenos Aires

In Spain:

Museo de Arte Contemporaneo, Madrid
Museo de Arte Moderno, Barcelona

In the United States:

Albion College, Albion, Michigan
American Life and Casualty Insurance Company,
 Fargo, North Dakota
American Republic Insurance Collection
American Trust & Savings, Dubuque, Iowa
Art Institute of Chicago, Chicago, Illinois
Art Institute of Los Angeles,
 Los Angeles, California
Art Museum of the New Britain Institute,
 New Britain, Connecticut
Ashland Oil Corporation, Ashland, Kentucky
Blanden Art Gallery, Fort Dodge, Iowa
Bloomington-Normal Art Association,
 Bloomington, Illinois
Bradley University, Peoria, Illinois
Brooklyn Museum, Brooklyn, New York
Bucknell University, Lewisburg, Pennsylvania
Carleton College, Northfield, Minnesota
Cedar Rapids Art Association,
 Cedar Rapids, Iowa
Cincinnati Art Museum, Cincinnati, Ohio
City Art Museum, St. Louis, Missouri
Cleveland Museum, Cleveland, Ohio
Colorado Springs Fine Art Center,
 Colorado Springs, Colorado

Davenport Museum, Davenport, Iowa
DePauw University, Greencastle, Indiana
Des Moines Art Center, Des Moines, Iowa
Detroit Institute of the Arts, Detroit, Michigan
Doane College, Crete, Nebraska
Dubuque Senior High School, Dubuque, Iowa
First National Bank, Iowa City, Iowa
First National Bank Collection,
 Tacoma, Washington
Flint Institute, Flint, Michigan
Honolulu Academy of Arts, Honolulu, Hawaii
Georgia State University, Atlanta, Georgia
Gettysburg College, Gettysburg, Pennsylvania
Indiana University, Bloomington, Indiana
International Business Machines Corporation,
 New York, New York
Iowa State Bank & Trust, Fairfield, Iowa
Iowa State Bank & Trust, Iowa City, Iowa
Iowa State University, Ames, Iowa
Iowa Wesleyan College, Mount Pleasant, Iowa
Joslyn Art Museum, Omaha, Nebraska
Library of Congress, Washington, D.C.
Lindenwood Colleges, St. Charles, Missouri
Louisiana State University,
 Baton Rouge, Louisiana
Luther College, Decorah, Iowa
Merchants National Bank, Cedar Rapids, Iowa
Mint Museum, Charlotte, North Carolina
Muscatine Museum, Muscatine, Iowa
Museum of Modern Art, New York, New York
National Gallery of Art, Washington, D.C.
New Jersey State Museum, Trenton, New Jersey
New York Public Library,
 New York, New York
Oakland Municipal Art Museum,
 Oakland, California
Ohio University, Athens, Ohio
Oklahoma Museum, Tulsa, Oklahoma
Pacific Lutheran University Collection,
 Tacoma, Washington
Pasadena Art Museum, Pasadena, California
Pennsylvania Academy of The Fine Arts,
 Philadelphia, Pennsylvania

Philadelphia Museum of Art,
   Philadelphia, Pennsylvania
Portland Art Museum, Portland, Oregon
R. M. Light and Company,
   Boston, Massachusetts
Rosenwald Collection, Jenkintown, Pennsylvania
Salt Lake Public Library, Salt Lake City, Utah
San Francisco Art Association,
   San Francisco, California
Seattle Museum, Seattle, Washington
Shenandoah Public Library, Shenandoah, Iowa
Silvermine Guild of Artists,
   New Canaan, Connecticut
Sioux City Art Museum, Sioux City, Iowa
Southern Illinois University, Carbondale, Illinois
Southwest Missouri State College, Springfield,
   Missouri
Springfield Art Museum, Springfield, Missouri
Starr King School for the Ministry, Berkeley,
   California
Syracuse University, Syracuse, New York
Tacoma Art Museum, Tacoma, Washington
Time Magazine, New York, New York
Topeka University, Topeka, Kansas
United States Information Agency for
   Exhibition in the Far East
University of Delaware, Newark, Delaware
University of Georgia, Athens, Georgia
University of Illinois, Urbana, Illinois
University of Iowa Museum of Art,
   Iowa City, Iowa
University of Maine Art Collection, Orono,
   Maine
University of Michigan Museum of Art,
   Ann Arbor, Michigan
University of Minnesota, Minneapolis,
   Minnesota
University of Nebraska, Lincoln, Nebraska
University of Northern Iowa, Cedar Falls, Iowa
University of Utah, Salt Lake City, Utah
University of Washington, Seattle, Washington
Walker Art Center, Minneapolis, Minnesota

Washington State University, Pullman,
   Washington
Washington University, St. Louis, Missouri
Waterloo Municipal Galleries, Waterloo, Iowa
Wesleyan University, Davison Art Center,
   Middletown, Connecticut
Whitney Museum of American Art,
   New York, New York
William Rockhill Nelson Gallery of Art,
   Kansas City, Missouri
Yale University, New Haven, Connecticut
In Other Countries:
American Embassy, Mexico
American Embassy, West Germany
Uffizi Gallery, Florence, Italy
Victoria Museum, Melbourne, Australia

Prizes and Awards

In Argentina: eighteen First Prizes

Since coming to the United States:

1944

First Prize:
17th International Exhibition of Prints,
   Seattle, Washington

1945

Purchase Prizes:
Library of Congress 3rd National Exhibition,
   Washington, D.C.
Philadelphia Print Club Exhibition,
   Philadelphia, Pennsylvania

1946

Purchase Prizes:
Denver Art Museum 52nd Annual Exhibition,
   Denver, Colorado
Des Moines Art Center Exhibition,
   Des Moines, Iowa
Philadelphia Print Club Exhibition,
   Philadelphia, Pennsylvania

1947

Purchase Prizes:
Denver Art Museum 53rd Annual Exhibition,
  Denver, Colorado
Walker Art Center Exhibition,
  Minneapolis, Minnesota
First Prize:
Iowa State Fair Art Salon, Des Moines, Iowa
Award:
Society of American Etchers and Engravers,
  New York, New York

1948

Purchase Prizes:
Brooklyn Museum 2nd National Print
  Exhibition, Brooklyn, New York
Indiana 1st Print and Drawing Exhibition,
  Bloomington, Indiana
Library of Congress 6th National Exhibition,
  Washington, D.C.
Northwest Printmakers Exhibition,
  Seattle, Washington
Philadelphia Print Club Exhibition,
  Philadelphia, Pennsylvania
Springfield Museum Exhibition,
  Springfield, Missouri
Alice McFadden Eyre Medal:
Pennsylvania Academy of The Fine Arts
  Exhibition, Philadelphia, Pennsylvania

1949

Purchase Prize:
Des Moines Art Center Exhibition,
  Des Moines, Iowa
Honorable Mention:
Joslyn Art Museum Central States Graphic Arts
  Exhibition, Omaha, Nebraska
1st and 2nd Awards:
Walker Art Center 2nd Biennial Exhibition,
  Minneapolis, Minnesota

1950

Purchase Prize:
Library of Congress 8th National Exhibition,
  Washington, D.C.
First Prize:
Iowa State Fair Art Salon Exhibition,
  Des Moines, Iowa
Honorable Mention:
Northwest Printmakers Exhibition,
  Seattle, Washington
Special Mention:
Joslyn Art Museum Exhibition,
  Omaha, Nebraska

1951

Purchase Prizes:
Des Moines Art Center 3rd Annual Exhibition,
  Des Moines, Iowa
Northwest Printmakers 23rd Annual Exhibition,
  Seattle, Washington
Springfield Art Museum Exhibition,
  Springfield, Missouri
Charles M. Lea Prize:
Philadelphia Print Club 28th Annual Exhibition,
  Philadelphia, Pennsylvania
Honorable Mention:
Bradley University National Exhibition,
  Peoria, Illinois
2nd Prize and Purchase:
Iowa State Fair Art Salon, Des Moines, Iowa

1952

Purchase Prizes:
Bradley University National Exhibition,
  Peoria, Illinois
Printmakers of Southern California 1st
  Exhibition, University of Southern California,
  Los Angeles, California
Edmunson Award:
Des Moines Art Center 4th Annual Exhibition,
  Des Moines, Iowa
Honorable Mention:
Joslyn Art Museum Midwest Biennial,
  Omaha, Nebraska

Award:
Nelson Gallery 3rd Mid-America Annual
    Exhibition, Kansas City, Missouri

1953

Honorable Mention:
Wichita Art Association 22nd Annual
    Exhibition, Wichita, Kansas
Special Commendation:
Des Moines Art Center 5th Annual Exhibition,
    Des Moines, Iowa

1955

Purchase Prizes:
Nelson Gallery 5th Mid-America Annual
    Exhibition, Kansas City, Missouri
Northwest Printmakers 27th International
    Exhibition, Seattle, Washington
Prize in Painting:
Des Moines Art Center 7th Annual Exhibition,
    Des Moines, Iowa
First Award:
Iowa State Fair Art Salon, Des Moines, Iowa

1956

Purchase Prize:
Library of Congress 14th National Exhibition,
    Washington, D.C.
Younkers Professional Award:
Des Moines Art Center 8th Annual Exhibition,
    Des Moines, Iowa

1957

Eyre Medal:
Pennsylvania Academy of The Fine Arts Annual
    Exhibition, Philadelphia, Pennsylvania
Purchase Prizes:
Des Moines Art Center 9th Annual Exhibition,
    Des Moines, Iowa
San Francisco Art Association Exhibition,
    San Francisco, California
Society of Washington Printmakers Exhibition,
    Washington, D.C.
Springfield Art Museum Exhibition,
    Springfield, Missouri

University of Northern Iowa, Cedar Falls, Iowa
Charles M. Lea Prize:
Philadelphia Print Club Exhibition,
    Philadelphia, Pennsylvania
Mention of Special Merit:
Bay Printmakers Society 3rd National
    Exhibition, Oakland, California
R. M. Light and Co. Purchase Prize:
Boston Printmakers 10th Annual Exhibition,
    Boston, Massachusetts

1958

Purchase Prizes:
Brooklyn Museum 11th National Print
    Exhibition, Brooklyn, New York
Des Moines Art Center 10th Annual Exhibition,
    Des Moines, Iowa
Pasadena Art Museum National Print
    Exhibition, Pasadena, California
Silvermine Guild 2nd National Print
    Exhibition, New Canaan, Connecticut
Springfield Art Museum 28th Annual
    Exhibition, Springfield, Missouri
Walker Art Center Biennial Exhibition,
    Minneapolis, Minnesota
Posada Award:
Primera Exposition Bienal Interamericana de
    Pintura y Grabado en Mexico, Mexico City,
    Mexico
Honorable Mention:
Nelson Gallery 8th Annual Mid-America
    Exhibition, Kansas City, Missouri

1959

Purchase Awards:
Contemporary American Printmakers, DePauw
    University, Greencastle, Indiana
Junior Gallery of Art, Louisville, Kentucky
Library of Congress 17th National Exhibition
    of Prints, Washington, D.C.
Northwest Printmakers 30th Annual
    International Exhibition, Seattle, Washington
Honorable Mention:
Nelson Gallery 9th Annual Mid-America
    Exhibition, Kansas City, Missouri

Special Commendation:
Des Moines Art Center 11th Annual,
  Des Moines, Iowa
Open Award:
California Society of Etchers Open Award,
  San Francisco, California

1960

Purchase Awards:
American Prints, Yale University,
  New Haven, Connecticut
Chicago Art Institute, Chicago, Illinois
8th Annual Bradley University National Print
  Show, Peoria, Illinois
Nelson Gallery 10th Annual Mid-America
  Exhibition, Kansas City, Missouri
First Prize for Best Work in Exhibition
  Irrespective of Medium:
Nelson Gallery 10th Annual Mid-America
  Exhibition, Kansas City, Missouri
First Prize in Prints:
Des Moines Art Center 12th Annual Iowa
  Artists Exhibition, Des Moines, Iowa
Second Prize in Painting:
Des Moines Art Center 12th Annual Iowa
  Artists Exhibition, Des Moines, Iowa
Mencion Especial Honorifica with Gold Medal:
Second International Biennial and One-Man
  Show *con salas de honor:* Painting, Sculpture
  and Prints, Palace of Fine Arts,
  Mexico City, Mexico

1961

Purchase Awards:
De Cordova Museum, Lincoln, Massachusetts
Luther College Fine Arts Festival, Decorah, Iowa
Northwest Printmakers 32nd International
  Exhibition, Seattle, Washington
Springfield Art Museum 31st Annual Exhibition,
  Springfield, Missouri
First Prize:
1961 Northeast Iowa Show, Cedar Falls, Iowa
Des Moines Art Center 13th Annual Iowa
  Artists Exhibition, Des Moines, Iowa

Honorable Mention and Invited Small
  One-Man Show:
Pennsylvania Academy of The Fine Arts
  156th Annual Exhibition, Philadelphia,
  Pennsylvania

1962

Purchase Awards:
Brooklyn Museum 13th National Print
  Exhibition, Brooklyn, New York
Des Moines Art Center 14th Annual Iowa
  Artists Show, Des Moines, Iowa
Library of Congress 18th Annual National
  Exhibition, Washington, D.C.
Nelson Gallery 12th Annual Mid-America
  Exhibition, Kansas City, Missouri
Oklahoma Printmakers Society Fourth National
  Exhibition, Oklahoma City Art Center,
  Oklahoma City, Oklahoma
Pasadena Art Museum, Pasadena, California
Ultimate Concerns, Westminster-Wesley
  Foundations, Ohio University, Athens, Ohio
Charles M. Lea Prize:
The Print Club, Philadelphia, Pennsylvania

1963

Purchase Awards:
Library of Congress 19th National Exhibition
  of Prints, Washington, D.C.
Otis Art Institute 2nd National Invitational
  Print Exhibition, Los Angeles, California
Honorable Mention:
Northwest Printmakers 34th International Print
  Exhibition, Seattle, Washington

1964

Purchase Award:
Luther College Fine Arts Festival, Decorah, Iowa
Award:
Juried Members Exhibition, The Print Club,
  Philadelphia, Pennsylvania

1965

Purchase Awards:

Waterloo Municipal Galleries 2nd Annual
   Art Show, Waterloo, Iowa

6th Annual National Ultimate Concerns,
   Westminster-Wesley Foundations, Ohio
   University, Athens, Ohio

Esther and Edith Younker Prize:
   Des Moines Art Center 17th Annual Iowa
   Artists Exhibition, Des Moines, Iowa

1966

Purchase Awards:

Carleton College Centennial Print Exhibit,
   Northfield, Minnesota

Des Moines Art Center 18th Annual Iowa
   Artists Exhibition, Des Moines, Iowa

1968

Purchase Award:

American Graphic Workshops '68,
   Cincinnati Art Museum, Cincinnati, Ohio

1970

First Prizes:

Color Prints of the Americas, New Jersey
   State Museum, Trenton, New Jersey

1st Biennal del Grabado, Latino Americano en
   San Juan de Puerto Rico,
   San Juan, Puerto Rico

Second International Biennial of Graphic Art,
   Florence, Italy

Special Mention:

Pan American Show of Prints and Drawings,
   Cali, Colombia

Purchase Award:

Lindenwood Colleges Fifth Invitational Exhibit,
   St. Charles, Missouri

1971

Bertha von Moschzisker Prize:

Philadelphia Print Club Annual Exhibition,
   Philadelphia, Pennsylvania

Purchase Prizes:

1st International Biennial of Graphic Arts,
   Honolulu, Hawaii

Georgia State University 2nd Annual National
   Print Exhibition, Atlanta, Georgia

Special Mention:

Exposicion Pan American de Artoc Graficas,
   Cali, Colombia

Purchase Awards:

Doane College Purchase Exhibition,
   Crete, Nebraska

Georgia State University 2nd Annual National
   Print Exhibition, Atlanta, Georgia

One-man Exhibitions

1945

San Francisco Museum of Art,
   San Francisco, California

Whyte Galleries, Washington, D.C.

1947

Buenos Aires, Argentina

Chicago Art Institute, Chicago, Illinois

1948

University of Louisville, Allen R. Hite Institute,
   Louisville, Kentucky

1949

Beloit College, Beloit, Wisconsin

Bowling Green State University,
   Bowling Green, Ohio

Carleton College, Northfield, Minnesota

College of William and Mary,
   Williamsburg, Virginia

Colorado Springs Fine Arts Center,
   Colorado Springs, Colorado

Cranbrook Academy of Fine Arts,
   Bloomfield Hills, Michigan

Des Moines Art Center, Des Moines, Iowa
Florida State University, Tallahassee, Florida
Milwaukee Art Institute, Milwaukee, Wisconsin
Museum of Fine Arts, Houston, Texas
Purdue University, Lafayette, Indiana
University of Delaware, Newark, Delaware
University of Iowa Museum of Art,
 Iowa City, Iowa
Walker Art Center, Minneapolis, Minnesota

1950

Currier Gallery of Art,
 Manchester, New Hampshire
Fairmont State College, Fairmont, West Virginia
Hollins College, Hollins College, Virginia
Mills College, Oakland, California
Nelson Gallery of Art, Kansas City, Missouri
Northwestern University, Evanston, Illinois
San Francisco Museum of Art,
 San Francisco, California
Santa Barbara Museum of Art,
 Santa Barbara, California
Scripps College, Claremont, California
Stanford University, Palo Alto, California
State University of New York at Oswego,
 Oswego, New York
University of Colorado, Boulder, Colorado
University of Kentucky, Lexington, Kentucky
University of Michigan, Ann Arbor, Michigan
University of Southern California,
 Los Angeles, California
University of Tennessee, Knoxville, Tennessee

1951

Arkansas State College, State College, Arkansas
Cornell University, Ithaca, New York
Coronet Theatre, Davenport, Iowa
Fort Dodge Federation of Arts,
 Fort Dodge, Iowa
Honolulu Academy of Arts, Honolulu, Hawaii
University of Manitoba, Winnipeg,
 Manitoba, Canada
University of Missouri, Columbia, Missouri

University of Nebraska, Lincoln, Nebraska
University of Oklahoma, Norman, Oklahoma

1952

Louisiana State University,
 Baton Rouge, Louisiana
Tulane University, New Orleans, Louisiana
University of Georgia, Athens, Georgia
University of Kentucky, Lexington, Kentucky
University of Wisconsin, Madison, Wisconsin

1953

Memphis Academy of Arts, Memphis, Tennessee

1954

Cedar Rapids Art Association,
 Cedar Rapids, Iowa
Museo de Arte Contemporaneo, Madrid, Spain
Museo de Arte Moderno, Barcelona, Spain

1957

Emory University, Atlanta, Georgia
Retrospective Exhibition, University of Iowa
 Museum of Art, Iowa City, Iowa

1958

Guest of Honor Exhibition, Oakland Art
 Museum, Oakland, California

1959

Latin American Traveling Show, "Intaglios"
 (one-man show with students of Lasansky),
 under the auspices of the United States
 Information Agency for a three-year period.
 The itinerary included the following locations:
Albright Art Gallery, Buffalo, New York
Art Museum, Mendoza, Argentina
Art Museum, Villa Maria, Argentina
Binational Center, Santiago, Chile
Instituto Peruana-Norteamericano de Culture,
 Lima, Peru
Museum of Fine Arts, Cordoba, Argentina
Museum of Fine Arts of the Provinces,
 La Plata, Argentina
Museum of Modern Art, Sao Paulo, Brazil
Municipal Museum of Fine Arts,
 Rosario, Argentina

National Museum of Fine Art, Buenos Aires
    (Latin American opening)
Retrospective Exhibition, University of Iowa
    Museum of Art, Iowa City, Iowa. Sponsored
    by the United States Information Agency

1960

Intaglios Show, Palace of Fine Arts,
    Mexico City, Mexico
Retrospective Exhibition awarded by the Ford
    Foundation and traveling under the auspices of
    the American Federation of Arts, 1960–1962:
Clarke College, Dubuque, Iowa
Des Moines Art Center, Des Moines, Iowa
Fort Dodge Federation of Arts,
    Fort Dodge, Iowa
Grinnell College, Grinnell, Iowa
Sanford Museum, Cherokee, Iowa
Sioux City Art Center, Sioux City, Iowa
University of Northern Iowa, Cedar Falls, Iowa
Waterloo Recreation Commission,
    Waterloo, Iowa

1961

Brooklyn Museum, Brooklyn, New York
Department of Art, University of California,
    Berkeley, California
Joslyn Art Museum, Omaha, Nebraska
Los Angeles County Museum,
    Los Angeles, California
Museum of Art, University of Oregon,
    Eugene, Oregon
Phoenix Art Museum, Phoenix, Arizona
School of Art, Syracuse University,
    Syracuse, New York
School of Painting, Ohio University,
    Athens, Ohio
Seattle Art Museum, Seattle, Washington
University of Wichita, Wichita, Kansas
Westmar College, LeMars, Iowa
Invited Small One-man Show: 156th Annual
    Exhibition Pennsylvania Academy of Fine Art,
    Philadelphia, Pennsylvania

1962

The Burlington Hawkeye, Burlington, Iowa

1965

Carleton College, Northfield, Minnesota
Southwest Missouri State College,
    Springfield, Missouri

1966

Declined invitation to exhibit in Rooms of
    Honor at 3rd Biennial of Fine Arts in
    Cordoba, Argentina

1966–67

The Nazi Drawings:
Des Moines Art Center, Des Moines, Iowa
Midwest Tour
Philadelphia Museum of Art,
    Philadelphia, Pennsylvania
University of Iowa Museum of Art,
    Iowa City, Iowa
Whitney Museum of Art, New York, New York

1967

Mauricio Lasansky: Selections From Thirty
    Years of Printmaking, Iowa State University,
    Ames, Iowa

1969

The Nazi Drawings, Palace of Fine Arts,
    Mexico City, Mexico

1970

The Nazi Drawings, University of Iowa
    Museum of Art, Iowa City, Iowa

1972

Dickinson College, Carlisle, Pennsylvania

1973

University of Georgia, Athens, Georgia
Blanden Art Gallery, Fort Dodge, Iowa

1974

The Nazi Drawings, Dickinson College,
    Carlisle, Pennsylvania

Invitational Exhibitions

1949

Exhibition of Current American Prints, Carnegie
Institute Museum of Art,
Pittsburgh, Pennsylvania

50 American Contemporary Prints,
Stillwater, Oklahoma

1951

Contemporary Art in the U.S., Worcester Art
Museum, Worcester, Massachusetts

Modern Print Masterpieces, Portland Art
Museum, Portland, Oregon

Sao Paulo Institute of Modern Art,
Sao Paulo, Brazil

University of Minnesota Invitational Print Show,
Minneapolis, Minnesota

1952

International Exhibition of Graphic Arts,
American Section, exhibited at Salzburg,
Vienna, Munich, Berlin, Hamburg

1953

Prints 1942–1952, Brooks Memorial Art Gallery,
Memphis, Tennessee

75 Living American Printmakers,
Fairfield, Connecticut

1954

Graphic Art USA, University of Illinois,
Urbana, Illinois

Graphics Invitational, Flint Institute of Arts,
Flint, Michigan

University of Minnesota Invitational Print
Show, Minneapolis, Minnesota

1955

Contemporary American Art, Museum of
Modern Art, Paris, France

El Arte Moderno en los Estados Unidos,
Barcelona, Spain

International Exposition of Contemporary
Gravure, Ljubljana, Yugoslavia

International Invitational Print Exhibition,
Washington University, St. Louis, Missouri

III Bienal Hispanoamericana de Arte,
Barcelona, Spain

1956

Contemporary American Printmakers,
University of Illinois, Urbana, Illinois

47 Midwestern Printmakers, 1020 Gallery,
Chicago, Illinois

20 American Printmakers, Michigan State
University, East Lansing, Michigan

Smithsonian Institute Traveling Show

The Butler Institute of American Art Mid-Year
Show, Youngstown, Ohio

1957

4th International Bordighera Biennale,
Bordighera, Italy

International Exposition of Contemporary
Gravure, Ljubljana, Yugoslavia

Palace of the Legion of Honor,
San Francisco, California

Regional Art Today, Joslyn Art Museum,
Omaha, Nebraska

Society of American Graphic Artists 41st
Annual Exhibition, New York, New York

10 Contemporary Printmakers,
Bloomington-Normal Art Association,
Bloomington, Illinois

University of Northern Iowa Invitational Print
Show, Cedar Falls, Iowa

University of Utah National Print and Drawing
Exhibition, Salt Lake City, Utah

1958

Midwestern University Printmakers Exhibition,
University of Kansas Museum of Art,
Lawrence, Kansas

Modern Master Prints, University of California,
Berkeley, California

Primera Exposition Bienal Interamericana de
Pintura y Grabado en Mexico,
Mexico City, Mexico

Recent American Prints, University of Illinois,
Urbana, Illinois

1959

Contemporary American Printmakers, DePauw University, Greencastle, Indiana

Eleven American Printmakers, Pennsylvania State University, University Park, Pennsylvania

Incisori Americani Contemporanei, Contemporary American Prints, organized by the Brooklyn Museum, Brooklyn, New York, to travel in Europe, 1959–1960

Junior Art Gallery, Louisville, Kentucky

100 American Works on Paper, Institute of Contemporary Art, Boston, Massachusetts

Pennsylvania Academy 154th Exhibition of Drawings, Paintings, and Prints, Philadelphia, Pennsylvania

Prints by College Artists-Teachers, Philadelphia Art Alliance, Philadelphia, Pennsylvania

1960

American Prints: 1950–1960, Yale University Art Gallery, New Haven, Connecticut

1960 International Biennial of Prints, Cincinnati Art Museum, Cincinnati, Ohio

Pennsylvania Academy 155th Exhibition of Drawings, Paintings, and Prints, Philadelphia, Pennsylvania

Second International Biennial, Palace of Fine Arts, Mexico City, Mexico

Three Masters of Intaglio, University of Kentucky, Lexington, Kentucky

1961

Eleventh Annual Mid-America Exhibition, Nelson Gallery, Kansas City, Missouri

50 American Printmakers, De Cordova and Dana Museum, Lincoln, Nebraska

1962

American Prints Today—1962, Print Council of America. Shown simultaneously in seven different cities, each show traveling for five months.

Invitational Exhibition of Intaglio and Lithographic Prints, The Print Club, Philadelphia, Pennsylvania

12th Annual Birmingham Festival of Arts, Birmingham, Alabama

1963

Contemporary Masters: Drawings and Prints, Annual Kane Memorial Exhibition, Providence, Rhode Island

Cultural Exchange Program to the Balkan Countries, sponsored by the United States Department of State

Fifth Exposition Internationale de Gravure, Ljubljana, Yugoslavia

Graphic Arts USA, Cultural Exchange Program to the USSR

Graphic Exhibition, Albertina, Vienna, Austria

Lasansky and His Students, sponsored by the United States Information Agency and the Palisades Foundation; on tour in Germany, Austria, and Italy

Sao Paulo Invitational Biennial, Sao Paulo, Brazil

2nd National Invitational Print Exhibition, Otis Art Institute of Los Angeles County, Los Angeles, California

The Fabulous Decade: Prints of the Nineteen Fifties, Philadelphia, Pennsylvania

1964

Graphic Art Exhibition, International Book Art Exhibition, Leipzig, German Democratic Republic

Juried Members Exhibition, The Print Club, Philadelphia, Pennsylvania

Sixth Exposition Internationale de Gravure, Ljubljana, Yugoslavia

1964–65

New York World's Fair, New York

1966

First International Biennial of Prints, Kracow, Poland

Prints: 1800–1945, Minneapolis Institute of Art, Minneapolis, Minnesota; City Art Museum, St. Louis, Missouri; 12 Major Printmakers, Los Angeles Valley College, Van Nuys, California

1967

Seventh Exposition Internationale de Gravure,
Ljubljana, Yugoslavia

The Artist as His Subject, Museum of Modern
Art, New York, New York

Vancouver Print International, in honor of the
Canadian Confederation Centennial,
Vancouver, British Columbia, Canada

1968

American Graphic Workshops '68, Cincinnati
Art Museum, Cincinnati, Ohio

American Prints, National Academy of Fine
Arts, Amsterdam, Holland

Lakeview Center for the Arts and Sciences,
Peoria, Illinois

Second International Biennial of Prints,
Kracow, Poland

16th National Print Exhibition
(20th Anniversary Show), Brooklyn Museum,
Brooklyn, New York

25 American Artists, The Hague, Holland

University of Northern Iowa, Cedar Falls, Iowa

1969

1st British International Print Show,
Bradford City, England

The Nazi Drawings, Palace of Fine Arts,
Mexico City, Mexico

Pacific Lutheran University,
Tacoma, Washington

1970

Brooklyn Print Show, Brooklyn, New York

Cedar Rapids Art Center, Cedar Rapids, Iowa

Color Prints of the Americas, New Jersey State
Museum, Trenton, New Jersey

1st Biennial del Grabado, Latino Americano en
San Juan de Puerto Rico, San Juan, Puerto Rico

International Biennial of Prints and Drawings,
Cali, Colombia

International Graphic Art 1945-1970,
Frechen, Germany

Iowa Wesleyan College, Mt. Pleasant, Iowa

Lindenwood Colleges, St. Charles, Missouri

2nd International Biennial of Graphic Art,
Florence, Italy

35th Biennial Art Exhibition, Venice, Italy

University of Iowa Museum of Art,
Iowa City, Iowa

1971

Biennial of the Moderna Galeria,
Ljubljana, Yugoslavia

1st International Biennial of Graphic Arts,
Honolulu, Hawaii

Graphic der Welt, Albertina Museum,
Vienna, Austria

International Biennial of Prints and Drawings,
Cali, Colombia

Oversize Prints, Whitney Museum,
New York, New York

1972

American Prints: '72, Iowa State University,
Ames, Iowa. Dedicated to Mauricio Lasansky's
27 years of teaching at The University of Iowa

International Print Biennial, Fredrikstad, Norway

Silvermine Guild of Artists,
New Canaan, Connecticut

2nd San Juan Biennial in Puerto Rico,
San Juan, Puerto Rico

3rd Biennial of Graphic Art, Palazzo Strozzi,
Florence, Italy

1973

American Prints 1973, Iowa State University,
Ames, Iowa

Georgia State University, Atlanta, Georgia

2nd American Biennial of Graphic Arts,
Cali, Colombia

The Innovators, an exhibition of nine works at
the Jane Haslem Gallery, Washington, D.C.

1974

3rd International Biennial Exhibition,
San Juan, Puerto Rico

Exhibition Chronology

1946

Denver Art Museum, 52nd Annual,
  Denver, Colorado
Library of Congress, 4th National,
  Washington, D.C.
Pennsylvania Academy of The Fine Arts
  Exhibition, Philadelphia, Pennsylvania
Wichita Art Association, 15th Annual,
  Wichita, Kansas

1947

Brooklyn Museum, Brooklyn, New York
Denver Art Museum, 53rd Annual,
  Denver, Colorado
Iowa State Fair Art Salon, Des Moines, Iowa
Library of Congress, Washington, D.C.
National Academy, 121st Annual Exhibition,
  New York, New York
Northwest Printmakers 9th Annual Exhibition,
  Seattle, Washington
Pennsylvania Academy of The Fine Arts,
  45th Annual Watercolor and Prints,
  Philadelphia, Pennsylvania
The Print Club,
  Philadelphia, Pennsylvania
San Francisco Museum of Art, 11th Annual
  Drawing and Print Exhibition,
  San Francisco, California
Society of American Etchers, Gravers,
  Lithographers & Woodcutters, 32nd Annual
  Exhibition, New York, New York
Walker Art Center, 1st Biennial,
  Minneapolis, Minnesota
Wichita Art Association, Wichita, Kansas

1948

American Color Print Society Annual,
  Philadelphia, Pennsylvania
Brooklyn Museum, Brooklyn, New York
Denver Art Museum, 54th Annual Show,
  Denver, Colorado

The Indiana First Print and Drawing Exhibition,
  Bloomington, Indiana
Laguna Beach Art Association, 7th Annual Print
  Exhibition, Laguna Beach, California
Library of Congress, Washington, D.C.
Northwest Printmakers 10th Annual Exhibition,
  Seattle, Washington
The Pennsylvania Academy of The Fine Arts,
  46th Annual Watercolor and Prints,
  Philadelphia, Pennsylvania

1949

Brooklyn Museum, Brooklyn, New York
Des Moines Art Center, Des Moines, Iowa
50 Contemporary American Prints,
  Stillwater, Oklahoma
Joslyn Art Museum, Second Graphic Arts
  Annual, Omaha, Nebraska
Library of Congress, Washington, D.C.
Northwest Printmakers 11th Annual Exhibition,
  Seattle, Washington
Philadelphia Art Alliance, The Artist Looks at
  Himself, Philadelphia, Pennsylvania
Philadelphia Watercolor and Prints 47th Annual,
  Philadelphia, Pennsylvania
The Print Club,
  Philadelphia, Pennsylvania
San Francisco Art Museum, 13th Annual,
  San Francisco, California
Springfield Art Museum, Springfield, Missouri
Walker Art Center, 2nd Biennial,
  Minneapolis, Minnesota

1950

Brooklyn Museum, Brooklyn, New York
Des Moines Art Center, Des Moines, Iowa
Iowa State Fair Art Salon, Des Moines, Iowa
Joslyn Art Museum, Midwest Show,
  Omaha, Nebraska
Laguna Beach Art Association,
  Laguna Beach, California
Library of Congress, Washington, D.C.

Northwest Printmakers 12th Annual Exhibition
Seattle, Washington
Philadelphia Watercolor and Prints 48th Annual,
Philadelphia, Pennsylvania
The Print Club,
Philadelphia, Pennsylvania
San Francisco Art Association,
San Francisco, California
Springfield Art Museum, Springfield, Missouri

1951

Brooklyn Museum, Brooklyn, New York
Colorado Springs Fine Arts Center, 13th Artists
West of the Mississippi,
Colorado Springs, Colorado
Coronet Theatre, Davenport, Iowa
Denver Art Museum, 57th Annual,
Denver, Colorado
Des Moines Art Center, Des Moines, Iowa
Iowa State Fair Art Salon, Des Moines, Iowa
Kansas State College, Fine Arts Festival,
Manhattan, Kansas
Library of Congress, Washington, D.C.
Northwest Printmakers 23rd International
Exhibition, Seattle, Washington
Philadelphia Water Color and Prints 49th
Annual, Philadelphia, Pennsylvania
Portland Art Museum, Modern Print
Masterpieces, Portland, Oregon
The Print Club, 28th Annual Exhibition,
Philadelphia, Pennsylvania
Salzburg Museum of Modern Art,
Salzburg, Austria
Sao Paulo Institute of Modern Art of Brazil,
Sao Paulo, Brazil
Society of American Etchers, Gravers,
Lithographers & Woodcutters, 35th
Annual Exhibition, New York, New York
Springfield Art Museum, 21st Annual,
Springfield, Missouri
United States Embassy, Cultural Relations
Service, Paris, France
University of Illinois, Group Show of Modern
American Printmakers, Urbana, Illinois
University of Minnesota, Invitational Show,
Minneapolis, Minnesota

University of Wichita, Wichita Invitational
Show, Wichita, Kansas
Worcester Art Museum, Contemporary Art in
the United States, Worcester, Massachusetts

1952

Bradley University, Peoria, Illinois
Brooklyn Museum, Brooklyn, New York
Denver Art Museum, Denver, Colorado
Exhibition Momentum, Chicago, Illinois
Indiana University, Invitational Show,
Bloomington, Indiana
Metropolitan Museum of Art, Drawings,
Watercolors and Prints, New York, New York
Midwest 2nd Biennial Exhibition, Joslyn Art
Museum, Omaha, Nebraska
Nelson Gallery, Mid-America Annual,
Kansas City, Missouri
Northwest Printmakers 24th International
Exhibition, Seattle, Washington
The Print Club, Philadelphia, Pennsylvania
San Francisco Museum of Art, 16th Annual of
Drawing and Prints, San Francisco, California
Springfield Art Museum, 22nd Annual
Exhibition, Springfield, Missouri
University of Georgia, Athens, Georgia
University of Southern California,
Printmakers of Southern California,
Los Angeles, California
Walker Art Center, 3rd Biennial of Painting
and Prints, Minneapolis, Minnesota

1953

American Federation of Arts Traveling Show,
selected from the Metropolitan Museum Show
American Federation of Arts Traveling Show,
selected from Pennsylvania Academy Annual
Ball State University, Muncie, Indiana
Brooks Memorial Art Gallery, Best 15
American Prints of the Last 10 years,
Memphis, Tennessee
Dallas Print Society, Dallas, Texas
Denver Art Museum, Denver, Colorado

1953

Des Moines Art Center, Des Moines, Iowa

Exhibition Momentum, Chicago, Illinois

Fort Wayne Art Museum, Fort Wayne, Indiana

Memphis Academy of Arts, University of
Arkansas, Fayetteville, Arkansas

Nelson Gallery, 2nd Mid-America Annual
Exhibition, Kansas City, Missouri

Ohio Wesleyan University, Delaware, Ohio

The Print Club, 13th Annual Exhibition,
Philadelphia, Pennsylvania

San Francisco Museum, Drawing and Print
Exhibition 17th Annual,
San Francisco, California

Second Print Annual, New Britain, Connecticut

75 Prints by 75 Living American Printmakers,
Fairfield, Connecticut

Springfield Art Museum, 23rd Annual
Exhibition, Springfield, Missouri

University of Southern California, Printmakers
of Southern California, Los Angeles, California

University of Wichita, Wichita, Kansas

Wichita Art Association, Wichita, Kansas

1954

Bradley University, Peoria, Illinois

Brooklyn Museum, Brooklyn, New York

Cedar Rapids Art Association,
Cedar Rapids, Iowa

Denver Art Museum, Denver, Colorado

Des Moines Art Center, Des Moines, Iowa

Flint Institute of Arts, Graphics Invitational,
Flint, Michigan

Joslyn Art Museum, Midwest 3rd Biennial
Exhibition, Omaha, Nebraska

Madison Art Association Exhibition of
Printmaking, Madison, Wisconsin

Millikin College, Decatur, Illinois

Nelson Gallery, 3rd Mid-America Annual
Exhibition, Kansas City, Missouri

Northwest Printmakers, 26th International
Exhibition, Seattle, Washington

University of Illinois, Graphic Art USA 1954,
Urbana, Illinois

University of Minnesota, Invitation Print Show,
Minneapolis, Minnesota

University of Southern California, Printmakers
of Southern California, Los Angeles, California

Walker Art Center, 4th Biennial of Painting
and Prints, Minneapolis, Minnesota

Youngstown College, College Prints 1954,
Youngstown, Ohio

1955

Bay Printmakers, First Annual,
Oakland, California

Boston Printmakers, 8th Annual Exhibition,
Boston, Massachusetts

Bradley University, Fifth Annual Exhibition,
Peoria, Illinois

Brooklyn Museum, Print Annual,
Brooklyn, New York

Des Moines Art Center, 7th Annual Artists
Show, Des Moines, Iowa

International Exposition of Contemporary
Gravure, Ljubljana, Yugoslavia

Iowa State Fair Art Salon, Des Moines, Iowa

Nelson Gallery, 5th Mid-America Annual
Exhibition, Kansas City, Missouri

Northwest Printmakers, 27th International
Exhibition, Seattle, Washington

Oakland Art Museum, Western Sculpture and
Print Exhibition, Oakland, California

The Print Club, 40th Anniversary
Exhibition, Philadelphia, Pennsylvania

Springfield Art Museum, 25th Annual
Exhibition, Springfield, Missouri

Washington University International Invitational
Print Exhibition, St. Louis, Missouri

Washington University Invitational,
St. Louis, Missouri

1956

Des Moines Art Center, Des Moines, Iowa

Joslyn Art Museum, Midwest 4th Biennial
Exhibition, Omaha, Nebraska

Library of Congress, Washington, D.C.

Michigan State University, 20 American
Printmakers, East Lansing, Michigan
Nelson Gallery, Mid-America Annual
Exhibition, Kansas City, Missouri
San Francisco Art Association, 19th Annual,
San Francisco, California
University of Illinois, 50 Contemporary
American Print Makers, Urbana, Illinois
Youngstown College Print Show.
Youngstown, Ohio

1957

Bay Printmakers Society, 3rd National
Exhibition of Prints, Oakland, California
Bloomington-Normal Art Association, Ten
Contemporary Printmakers,
Bloomington, Illinois
Boston Printmakers, 10th Annual Exhibition,
Boston, Massachusetts
California School of Fine Arts, The Printmaker
1450–1950, Otis Art Institute,
Los Angeles, California
Des Moines Art Center, 9th Annual Iowa
Artists Show, Des Moines, Iowa
Emory University, Atlanta, Georgia
4th International Bordighera Biennial,
Bordighera, Italy
Iowa State Fair Art Salon, Des Moines, Iowa
Joslyn Art Museum, Regional Art Today,
Omaha, Nebraska
Library of Congress, 15th National Exhibition
of Prints, Washington, D.C.
Nelson Gallery, Mid-America Annual
Exhibition, Kansas City, Missouri
Northwest Printmakers, 28th International
Exhibition, Seattle, Washington
Pennsylvania Academy of The Fine Arts,
152nd Annual Exhibition,
Philadelphia, Pennsylvania
The Print Club, 34th Annual Exhibition of
Etching, Philadelphia, Pennsylvania
San Francisco Art Association, 21st Annual
Exhibition, San Francisco, California
Smithsonian Institute, Society of Washington
Printmakers, Washington, D.C.

Springfield Art Museum, 27th Annual
Exhibition, Springfield, Missouri
University of Northern Iowa, Cedar Falls, Iowa

1958

Brooklyn Museum, 11th National Print
Exhibition, Brooklyn, New York
Des Moines Art Center, 10th Annual Iowa
Artists Show, Des Moines, Iowa
Denver Art Museum, 64th Annual Exhibition,
Denver, Colorado
Iowa State Fair Art Salon, Des Moines, Iowa
Joslyn Art Museum, Midwest 5th Biennial
Exhibition, Omaha, Nebraska
Junior Art Gallery, Louisville, Kentucky
Library of Congress, 16th National Exhibition
of Prints, Washington, D.C.
Nelson Gallery, 8th Annual Mid-America
Exhibition, Kansas City, Missouri
Pasadena Art Museum, National Print
Exhibition, Pasadena, California
Primera Exposicion de Obras Premiadas y
Seccion Grabado del 46 Salon Nacional de
Artes Plasticas, Argentina
The Print Club, 35th Annual Exhibition of
Prints, Philadelphia, Pennsylvania
Silvermine Guild of Artists, 2nd National Print
Exhibition, New Canaan, Connecticut
Smithsonian Institute, Society of Washington
Printmakers, Washington, D.C.
Springfield Art Museum, 28th Annual
Exhibition, Springfield, Missouri
University of California, Modern Master Prints
Exhibition, Berkeley, California
University of Illinois, 3rd Biennial Invitational
Exhibition, Urbana, Illinois
University of Kansas, Midwestern University
Printmakers Exhibition, Lawrence, Kansas

1959

Bay Printmakers Society, 5th National
Exhibition, San Francisco, California

Boston Printmakers, 12th Annual Exhibition,
Boston, Massachusetts

Butler Art Institute, Youngstown, Ohio

California Society of Etchers, 44th Annual Print
Exhibition, San Francisco, California

Denver Art Museum, 65th Annual,
Denver, Colorado

DePauw University Art Center, Contemporary
American Printmakers Exhibition,
Greencastle, Indiana

Des Moines Art Center, 11th Annual Iowa
Artists Show, Des Moines, Iowa

Iowa State Fair Art Salon, Des Moines, Iowa

Library of Congress, 17th National Exhibition
of Prints, Washington, D.C.

Luther College, Fine Arts Festival,
Decorah, Iowa

Nelson Gallery, 9th Annual Mid-America
Exhibition, Kansas City, Missouri

Northwest Printmakers, 30th International
Exhibition, Seattle, Washington

Pennsylvania Academy of The Fine Arts,
154th Annual Exhibition of Water Colors,
Prints and Paintings,
Philadelphia, Pennsylvania

The Print Club, 36th Annual Exhibition
of Etching and Engraving,
Philadelphia, Pennsylvania

Prints by College Art Teachers, Philadelphia
Art Alliance, Philadelphia, Pennsylvania

Springfield Art Museum, 29th Annual
Exhibition, Springfield, Missouri

1960

Brooklyn Museum, 12th National Print Annual,
Brooklyn, New York

Des Moines Art Center, 12th Annual Exhibition,
Des Moines, Iowa

Joslyn Art Museum, Midwest 6th Biennial,
Omaha, Nebraska

Luther College, Fine Arts Festival,
Decorah, Iowa

Nelson Gallery, Mid-America Annual
Exhibition, Kansas City, Missouri

Northwest Printmakers, 31st International
Exhibition, Seattle, Washington

The Print Club, Annual Exhibition of
Etching and Engraving,
Philadelphia, Pennsylvania

2nd National Biennial, National Print
Exhibition, Pasadena, California

Silvermine Guild of Artists,
New Canaan, Connecticut

Smithsonian Institution, 23rd National
Exhibition, Washington, D.C.

Springfield Art Museum, 30th Annual
Exhibition, Springfield, Missouri

1961

Luther College, Fine Arts Festival,
Decorah, Iowa

Northwest Iowa Show, Cedar Falls, Iowa

Northwest Printmakers, 32nd International
Exhibition, Seattle, Washington

San Francisco Art Association, Annual Drawing,
Print and Sculpture Exhibition,
San Francisco, California

Springfield Art Museum, 31st Annual
Exhibition, Springfield, Missouri

Ultimate Concerns, 2nd National Exhibition,
Ohio University Gallery, Athens, Ohio

1962

Brooklyn Museum, 13th National Print
Exhibition, Brooklyn, New York

Des Moines Art Center, 14th Annual Iowa
Artists Show, Des Moines, Iowa

Joslyn Art Museum, 7th Midwest Biennial,
Omaha, Nebraska

Luther College, Fine Arts Festival,
Decorah, Iowa

National Gallery, Printmakers 24th Exhibition,
Washington, D.C.

Pasadena Art Museum, 3rd Biennial National
Print Exhibition, Pasadena, California

Silvermine Guild of Artists, 4th National Print
Exhibition, New Canaan, Connecticut

Ultimate Concerns, Prints and Drawings,
Athens, Ohio

1963

Des Moines Art Center, 15th Annual Iowa
Artists Show, Des Moines, Iowa
Library of Congress, 19th National Exhibition
of Prints, Washington, D.C.
Nelson Gallery, Mid-America Annual
Exhibition, Kansas City, Missouri
Northwest Printmakers, 34th International
Exhibition, Seattle, Washington
Otis Art Institute, 2nd National Invitational
Print Exhibition, Los Angeles, California
Springfield Art Museum, 33rd Annual
Exhibition, Springfield, Missouri
Ultimate Concerns, Prints and Drawings,
Athens, Ohio

1964

Brooklyn Museum, 14th National Print
Exhibition, Brooklyn, New York
California Society of Etchers, Original Prints,
San Francisco, California
Des Moines Art Center, 16th Annual Iowa
Artists Exhibition, Des Moines, Iowa
International Triennial of Original Colored
Graphics, Grenchen, Switzerland
Luther College, Fine Arts Festival,
Decorah, Iowa

1965

Des Moines Art Center, 17th Annual Iowa
Artists Exhibition, Des Moines, Iowa
San Francisco Art Institute, 84th Annual
Exhibition, San Francisco, California

1966

Brooklyn Museum, 15th National Print
Exhibition, Brooklyn, New York
Joslyn Art Museum, 9th Midwest Biennial,
Omaha, Nebraska

Library of Congress, Washington, D.C.
Silvermine Guild of Artists, 6th National Print
Exhibition, New Canaan, Connecticut
Springfield Art Museum, 36th Annual
Exhibition, Springfield, Missouri
Ultimate Concerns, 7th National Prints and
Drawings Exhibition, Athens, Ohio

1967

Des Moines Art Center, 19th Annual
Exhibition of Iowa Artists, Des Moines, Iowa
Herron School of Art, Young Printmakers
1967, Indianapolis, Indiana
Northwest Printmakers, 38th Annual
International Exhibition, Seattle, Washington
Waterloo Municipal Galleries, 3rd Annual
Art Show, Waterloo, Iowa

1968

Brooklyn Museum, Brooklyn, New York
Cincinnati Art Museum, American Graphic
Workshops '68, Cincinnati, Ohio
Lakeview Center for the Arts and Sciences,
Peoria, Illinois
National Academy of the Fine Arts, American
Prints, Amsterdam, Holland
Second International Biennial of Prints,
Kracow, Poland
16th National Print Exhibition (20th anniversary
show) 25 American Artists,
The Hague, Holland
University of Northern Iowa,
Cedar Falls, Iowa

1969

1st British International Print Show,
Bradford City, England
Pacific Lutheran University,
Tacoma, Washington
Palace of Fine Arts, The Nazi Drawings,
Mexico City, Mexico

1970

1st San Juan Biennial in Puerto Rico,
  San Juan, Puerto Rico
Lindenwood Colleges, 5th Invitational Exhibit,
  St. Charles, Missouri
New Jersey State Museum, Color Prints of
  the Americas, Trenton, New Jersey
Pan American Show of Prints and Drawings,
  Cali, Colombia
2nd International Biennial of Graphic Art,
  Florence, Italy
35th Biennial Art Exhibition, Venice, Italy
University of Iowa Museum of Art, The Nazi
  Drawings, Iowa City, Iowa

1971

Albertina Museum, Graphic der Welt,
  Vienna, Austria
Biennial of the Moderna Galerica,
  Ljubljana, Yugoslavia
Doane College Purchase Exhibition,
  Crete, Nebraska
Exposicion Pan American de Artoc Graficas,
  Cali, Colombia
1st International Biennial of Graphic Arts,
  Honolulu, Hawaii
Georgia State University, 2nd Annual National
  Print Exhibition, Atlanta, Georgia
International Biennial of Prints and Drawings,
  Cali, Colombia
The Print Club, Annual Exhibition,
  Philadelphia, Pennsylvania

1972

Dickinson College, Carlisle, Pennsylvania
International Print Biennial,
  Fredrikstad, Norway
Iowa State University, American Prints: '72,
  Ames, Iowa
Palazzo Strozzi, 3rd Biennial of Graphic Arts,
  Florence, Italy
2nd San Juan Biennial in Puerto Rico,
  San Juan, Puerto Rico

Silvermine Guild of Arts,
  New Canaan, Connecticut

1973

Blanden Art Gallery, Fort Dodge, Iowa
Georgia State University, Atlanta, Georgia
Iowa State University, American Prints: '73,
  Ames, Iowa
Jane Haslem Gallery, The Innovators,
  Washington, D.C.
2nd American Biennial of Graphic Arts,
  Cali, Colombia

1974

Dickinson College, The Nazi Drawings,
  Carlisle, Pennsylvania
3rd San Juan Biennial in Puerto Rico,
  San Juan, Puerto Rico

Catalogues of Exhibitions

Albright Art Gallery, Buffalo, New York. 1959.
  *Intaglios—The Work of Mauricio Lasansky and
  Other Printmakers Who Studied with Him at
  The State University of Iowa.* Prepared by
  William Friedman under a grant from the
  United States Information Agency, with text
  in English, Spanish, and Portuguese.
American Federation of Arts, New York,
  New York. 1960. *Mauricio Lasansky.*
  Foreword by Carl Zigrosser.
Blanden Art Gallery, Fort Dodge, Iowa. 1973.
  *The Thematic Context of Mauricio Lasansky's
  Prints: 43 Prints—1937–1972.* Essay by
  Stephen Rhodes.
Brooklyn Museum, Brooklyn, New York. 1956.
  Ten Years of American Prints: 1947–1956.
  Essay by Una E. Johnson.

Dickinson College, Dickinson, Pennsylvania.
1972. *Mauricio Lasansky—Lasansky and Abstract Expressionism.* Essay by Michael Danoff.

Galeria Sintonia, Buenos Aires, Argentina. 1948. *Lasansky Exposicion de Grabados.* "Sobre la Obra de Lasansky" by Julio E. Payro.

International Biennial of Graphic Arts. 1970. San Juan, Puerto Rico.

Museum of Contemporary Art, Madrid, Spain. 1954. *Grabados de 1935–1953 Lasansky.* Introduction by Angel Ferrant.

Palace of Fine Arts, Mexico City, Mexico. 1969. *The Nazi Drawings.* Introduction by Edwin Honing.

Philadelphia Museum of Art, Philadelphia, Pennsylvania. 1966. *The Nazi Drawings.* Introduction by Edwin Honing.

Palazzo Strozzi, Florence, Italy. 1969. *2nd International Biennial of Prints.* Introduction to Lasansky by Gustave von Groschwitz.

University of Iowa, Iowa City, Iowa. 1957. *Lasansky: Twenty-four Years of Printmaking.* Introduction by Lester Longman.

Walker Art Center, Minneapolis, Minnesota. 1949. *A New Direction in Intaglio: The Work of Mauricio Lasansky and His Students.* Text by Lester Longman and William Friedman.

Whyte Gallery. Washington, D.C. 1944. *Engravings, Line-Cuts, Drypoints, Etchings, Lithographs by Mauricio Lasansky.* Introduction by Stanley Harter.

A Selected Bibliography

Arnold, Paul. "The Influence of Lasansky on Printmaking in the United States." Master of Fine Arts Thesis, University of Minnesota, 1955.

Archie, David. "Lasansky." *The Iowan Magazine,* January 1958.

————. "Lasansky, As Big As Life." *The Iowan Magazine,* February-March, 1960.

"The Artists' America." In *The American Heritage.* 4th ed. 1970.

Buckland-Wright, John. *Etching and Engraving.* New York, 1953.

Campofiorito, Quirino. "Artes Plasticas— Lasansky E Mais 37 Gravadores." *O Jornal* (Rio de Janiero), 4 February 1960.

Cohen, Henning. "Visions of Depravity." *The Reporter,* 4 May 1967.

Edmondson, L. *Etching.* New York, 1972.

Encyclopaedia Britannica. 1965. S.v. "Engraving."

Encyclopaedia Britannica. 1972. S.v. "Modern Printmaking."

"Exposición en Bellas Artes." *Impacto* (Mexico City), 26 February 1969.

"Flourishing Printmakers." *Time,* 1 February 1963.

Foss, Helen. "Lasansky Print Group: A New Direction in Printmaking." *College Art Journal* 8 (1949).

Frank, Waldo. *South American Journey.* New York, 1943.

Gesuldo, Vincente. *Encyclopedia Del Arte on America.* 1970.

Getlein, Frank, and Getlein, Dorothy. *The Bite of the Print.* New York, 1963.

Gilbert, Creighton. "Lasansky and the Hayter Circle." *Perspective* 1 (Washington University, St. Louis, 1948).

Glueck, Grace. "Non Fairy Tale." *New York Times,* 26 March 1967.

Goldman, Juliet. "Lasansky." *American Artist Magazine,* March 1970.

Gottfried, Lindemann. *Prints and Drawings: A Pictorial History.* New York, 1970.

Gual, Enrique F. "Dibujos Nazis." *Excelsior* (Mexico City), January 1969.

Haight, Anne Lyon. *Portrait of Latin America as Seen by Her Printmakers*. New York, 1946.

Hayter, Stanley William. *About Prints*. New York, 1962.

Hayter, Stanley William. *New Ways of Gravure*. New York, 1949.

Heller, Jules. *Printmaking*. New York, 1957.

Heller, Jules. *Printmaking Today*. New York, 1972.

Holland, Frank. "Modern Master's Prints Shown." *Chicago Sun-Times*, 13 March 1960.

Hooten, Bruce, and Kaiden, Mina. *Mother and Child in Modern Art*. New York, 1964.

"Iowa's Printmaker." *Time*, 1 December 1961.

J. G. "Modern Argentinian at Whyte Gallery, Washington." *Art Digest* 18 (1944).

Jordao, Pacheco. "Gravuras de Mauricio Lasansky." *O Globo* (Rio de Janiero), 5 February 1960.

Frommhold, Erhard. *Kunst in Widerstand*. Dresden, 1968.

Frommhold, Erhard. *Arte Della Resistenza 1922–1945*. Milan, 1970.

Lieberman, William. *Masters of Modern Art*. New York, 1954.

Lowengrund, Margaret. "Duplicate Lasansky Shows at Walker Art Center and Colorado Springs Fine Art Center." *Art Digest* 23 (1949).

Mallo, Jeronimo. "Mauricio Lasansky Artista y Maestro." *Cuadernos Americanos* 20 (1961).

"Mauricio Lasansky y sus Discipulos." *La Nacion* (Buenos Aires), 19 November 1959.

Mindelowitz, Daniel M. *A History of American Art*. Palo Alto, 1970.

Muller, Earl. *The Art of the Print*. New York, 1970.

"Nameless Evil." *Time*, 31 March 1967.

Neuvillate, Alfonso. "Los Dibujos Nazi de Mauricio Lasansky." *El Heraldo* (Mexico City), 18 January 1969.

Newland, Randa. "The Iowa Print Group After 25 Years." Master's thesis, University of Iowa, 1972.

Norris, Hoak. "A Cold Look at Horror." *Chicago Daily News*, 29 April 1970.

Ochs, James L. "The Technique and Printing of Lasansky's *Quetzalcoatl*." M.F.A. thesis, University of Iowa, 1974.

Pagano, Jose Leon. *Historia del Arte Argentino*. Buenos Aires, 1944.

"Paperbacks of Painting." *Time*, 2 June 1971.

Payro, Julio E. "Mauricio Lasansky." *Sur* (Buenos Aires), September 1948.

Peterdi, Gabor. *Printing—Old and New Methods*. New York, 1959.

"Portrait of the Artist." *Art News and Review* 3 (London, 1951).

Prize Winning Graphics. Fort Lauderdale, 1962.

Prize Winning Graphics, II. Fort Lauderdale, 1963.

Reese, Albert. *American Prize Prints of the Twentieth Century*. New York, 1949.

Ribeiro, Flexa. "Lasansky e a gravura Americana." *Jornal do Commercio* (Rio de Janiero), 24 January 1960.

Saavedra, Cornelio L. "El Arte De Lasansky." *Cordoba* (Cordoba, Argentina), September 1939.

Saavedra, Luis A. "Los Dibujos del Horror Nazi." *El Mercurio* (Santiago, Chile), 6 February 1969.

Seldis, Henry J. "Lasansky: License and Liberty Are Different." *Los Angeles Times*, 4 June 1961.

Shikes, Ralph E. *The Indignant Eye: The Artist as Social Critic in Prints and Drawings from the Fifteenth Century to Picasso*. (Boston, 1969).

Sieber, Roy. "Lasansky and the Iowa Print Group." *Print* 7 (1952).

Stinson, Robert E. "Mauricio Lasansky: A Monograph." Master's thesis, University of Iowa, 1948.

Stubbe, Wolf. *Graphic Arts in the Twentieth Century.* New York, 1963.

Taxier, Carol. "Mauricio Lasansky Artist-Teacher." *Impression,* Spring 1958.

Tibol, Raquel. "Estimaciones y Sobreestimaciones de Mauricio Lasansky." *Excelsior* (Mexico City), 17 June 1960.
_____. "Mauricio Lasansky." *Sintesis* (Mexico, D.F.), July 1959.
_____. "The Anti-Nazizme as Subject of Modern Art." *Calli,* March 1967.

"Un Artista Argentino en los EE. UU." *Life en Espanol,* 4 September 1961.

Vieira, Jose Geraldo. "Lasansky e seus discipulos." *Felha de Sao Paulo,* 3 April 1960.

A Visual Dictionary of Art: 1972. London, 1972.

Vivanco, Luis Philipe. "La Obra Grabada de Mauricio Lasansky." *Revista* (Barcelona), April 1954.

Willard, Charlotte. "Drawings from Hell." *Look,* 21 February 1967.
_____. "Lest We Forget." *New York Post,* 25 March 1967.

Zigrosser, Carl. "American Prints Since 1926: A Complete Revolution in the Making." *Art Digest,* November 1951.
_____. *What Is an Original Print?* Print Council of America, 1967.
_____. *Prints and Their Creators—A World History.* New York, 1974.

Prints are reproduced from the collection of
Emilia Barragan. Acknowledgment is also made to
Webster B. and Gloria Gelman for their interest and assistance.
The book was designed by Sam Maitin, with
photographs by Alfred J. Wyatt. The typeface is
Bembo Monotype, set by W. T. Armstrong, Inc.
The book was printed by Meriden Gravure.